Richard Price

Sermons on the Christian Doctrine as received by the different Denominations of Christians

Richard Price

Sermons on the Christian Doctrine as received by the different Denominations of Christians

ISBN/EAN: 9783337169763

Printed in Europe, USA, Canada, Australia, Japan

Cover: Foto ©Lupo / pixelio.de

More available books at **www.hansebooks.com**

SERMONS

ON THE

CHRISTIAN DOCTRINE

AS RECEIVED BY THE

DIFFERENT DENOMINATIONS

OF

CHRISTIANS.

TO WHICH ARE ADDED,

SERMONS

ON THE

SECURITY AND HAPPINESS

OF A

VIRTUOUS COURSE,

ON THE

GOODNESS OF GOD,

AND THE

RESURRECTION OF LAZARUS.

By RICHARD PRICE, D.D. LL.D. F.R.S.
And Fellow of the AMERICAN Philofophical Societies at
PHILADELPHIA and BOSTON.

DUBLIN:
Printed by JOHN EXSHAW, Nº. 98, Grafton-Street.
MDCCLXXXVII.

TO

THE CONGREGATION OF

PROTESTANT DISSENTERS

ASSEMBLING AT THE

GRAVEL-PIT MEETING-HOUSE

IN HACKNEY,

THESE DISCOURSES,

PUBLISHED AT THEIR REQUEST,

ARE DEDICATED,

BY THEIR OBLIGED

AND AFFECTIONATE PASTOR,

RICHARD PRICE.

ADVERTISEMENT.

BEFORE the Reader enters on the following Discourses, I think it necessary to acquaint him, that, being determined not to engage in Controversy, I shall make no reply to any Animadversions on the account which, in the first five of them, I have given of the Doctrines of Christianity; except, by acknowledging the mistakes into which I may have fallen, when convinced of them.

NEWINGTON GREEN,
Nov. 24, 1786.

CONTENTS.

SERMON I.

Of the Christian Doctrine as held by all Christians - Page 1.
From 1 Tim. i. 11.
The glorious gospel of the blessed God.

SERMON II.

Of the Christian Doctrine as held by *Trinitarians* and *Calvinists*. - Page 28.
From the same text.

SERMON III.

Of the Christian Doctrine as held by *Unitarians* and *Socinians*. - Page 69.
From the same text.

SERMON IV.

Of the PRE-EXISTENCE and DIGNITY of Chrift. - - - Page 105.

From 1 JOHN iv. 14.

We have feen and do teftify, that the Father fent the Son to be the Saviour of the world.

SERMON V.

Of the character of Chrift as the SAVIOUR OF THE WORLD. - Page 157.

From the fame text.

SERMON VI.

Of the SECURITY of a Virtuous Courfe.

Page 201.

From PROV. x. 9.

He that walketh uprightly, walketh furely.

SERMON VII.

Of the HAPPINESS of a Virtuous Courfe.

Page 227.

From

CONTENTS.

From Prov. ii. 17.

Her ways are ways of pleasantness, and all her paths are peace. She is a tree of life to them that lay hold of her; and happy is every one who receiveth her.

SERMON VIII. and IX.

Of the GOODNESS OF GOD. - Page 259.

From Psal. xxxiv. 8.

O taste and see that the Lord is good. Blessed is the man that trusteth in him.

SERMON X.

Of the RESURRECTION OF LAZARUS.

Page 321.

From John xi. 43, 44.

And when he had thus spoken, he cried with a loud voice, LAZARUS, COME FORTH. *And he that was dead came forth bound hand and foot with grave-clothes. And his face was bound about with a napkin. Jesus says to them; Loose him, and let him go.*

SERMON I.

OF THE CHRISTIAN DOCTRINE AS HELD BY ALL CHRISIANS.

1 TIM. i. 11.

The glorious gospel of the blessed God.

WE are all agreed in applying to the religion we profess the character of it given by St. Paul in these words. It is *the glorious Gospel of the blessed God.* It is a heavenly gift, important and interesting in the highest degree. Nothing, therefore, can be more proper than that we should examine it carefully, and endeavour to understand clearly its nature and contents. All our attachment to it without this must be unmeaning and absurd. My present design is to give you some assistance in making this examination, by anfwering in the beft manner I can the following enquiries.

What *is* the Gofpel? What inftruction does it convey? What is the information which renders it a GLORIOUS GOSPEL worthy of the bleffed God?

THE word *Gofpel*, as you well know, is derived, both in the *Englifh* and the *Greek* languages, from two words which fignify GOOD NEWS. The very title given it, therefore, in my text intimates to us its general nature and defign. It is a communication of good tidings to mankind from the bleffed God.

Before I enter upon an account of the particulars of this information, my views in this and fome following difcourfes require me to obferve to you, that there is a great diverfity of opinions among chriftians on this fubject. The different accounts which have been given of the Gofpel of Chrift are indeed numberlefs
and

and they have given rife to many great evils; particularly, the two following.

Firſt. An objection to Chriſtianity has been founded upon them on which great ſtreſs has been laid; and which, I fear, has prevented ſome from giving the evidence for it a patient, and favourable hearing. It has been urged that, if the Goſpel was indeed a revelation from heaven, it would be ſo clear and explicit as to leave no room for ſuch differences, and to preclude all diſputes about its meaning, a *dark* revelation being, as unbelievers ſay, an inconſiſtency, which implies a reflection on the perfections of the Deity, and equivalent to *no* revelation. Thoſe who make this objection go upon the ſuppoſition, that God can be the author of no information which is capable of being miſunderſtood, and conſequently of creating diſputes. There cannot be a more groundleſs ſuppoſition. God conveys information to us by our *reaſon* as well as by *revelation*. The light of nature is a light

light derived from him as well as the light of the Gospel; and there is no more reason to expect that the one should be so clear as to exclude mistakes and disputes than the other. While we continue such frail and fallible creatures as we are, it is impossible that we should not be in danger of falling into differences of opinion, and sometimes into gross errors; and to complain of this would be much the same with complaining because we are not made omniscient and perfect beings. There is not a principle of common sense that has not been controverted, nor a truth discoverable by the light of reason of which different accounts have not been given, and which has not been misconceived and perverted. And yet no one ever thinks of inferring from hence that reason is not the gift of God, or that it is not a valuable gift. There is just as little reason for drawing the like inference concerning Christianity from the

the different opinions and the disputes among its professors.

But there is another answer to this objection which is more to my present purpose; and which I shall take notice of, after mentioning the next great evil arising from the disputes among Christians. I mean; the embarrassments they occasion in the minds of many good men.

It is impossible, when plain and honest men hear the different parties among Christians contradicting one another in the manner they do; one saying, *this* is the Gospel of Christ; and another saying the contrary; and all positive and dogmatical: it is, I say, impossible that, in such circumstances, a plain man unaccustomed to enquiry should not be puzzled, and thrown into a state of perplexity and distraction. Most of these parties lay the greatest stress on their accounts of the Gospel; and too many go so far as to connect *salvation* with them, and to consign to hell all that do not receive them. I should do an essential service could I remove the stumbling-blocks which these litigations throw in the way of common Christians. And my chief intention in the present discourse is to attempt this, by shewing you that Christians of all parties, however they may censure one another, and whatever opposition there may seem to be in their sentiments, are agreed in all that is essential to Christianity, and with respect to all the information which it is its principal design to communicate. Should this appear, it will set our minds at ease amidst the controversies that take place in the Christian church, and enable us to look with an equal eye of charity and candour on all our fellow-christians: and it will also effectually remove that objection to Christianity which I have mentioned.

In attempting this, I will recite to you those doctrines and facts of Christianity which all Christians believe, and which are

are so plainly revealed as to exclude the possibility of disputes about them; after which, I will shew you the nature of the differences among Christians, in order to prove that the doctrines universally received are all that are essential.

In the first place; the Gospel teaches us that there is only one living and true God. This is a fundamental doctrine which the New Testament holds forth to us in almost every page. There is but *one* being good, says Jesus Christ, that is God. There are, says St. Paul, *Gods many; but to us there is but one God, the father.* Many of our fellow-christians, indeed, maintain doctrines which seem to clash with this essential doctrine; but they all profess to believe it, and with so much zeal as to be greatly offended whenever they are charged with contradicting it. Though the Divine nature, according to them, consists of *three persons*; and the Son (one of these *persons*) consists of *two natures*; yet these *three persons* make but

one

one being. If there is a palpable abſurdity in this, it only proves that the Goſpel teaches the Divine Unity ſo deciſively as to force every Chriſtian to acknowledge it, however inconſiſtent with his other opinions his acknowledgment of it may be.

But farther; the Goſpel teaches us, with perfect clearneſs, that this one God is poſſeſſed of all poſſible perfection; that he is infinitely wiſe, powerful, righteous, and benevolent; that he is the moral governor of the world, an enemy to all wickedneſs, and a friend to all goodneſs; and that he directs all events by his providence ſo particularly as that the hairs of our head are all numbered, and that a ſparrow does not fall to the ground without him. It teaches us alſo to imitate, to ſerve, and to worſhip him, and to put our truſt in him; and comprehends the whole of our duty in loving him with all our hearts, and in loving our neighbour as ourſelves. It declares to us the necessity of repentance and a holy life; a future state of rewards and punishments; and a future period of universal retribution when all mankind shall be judged according to their works.

There are no doubts about any of these particulars among Christians; and they include all that it is most necessary for us to know. But the doctrines which most properly constitute the Gospel are those which relate to Jesus Christ and his mediation. Here, also, there is an agreement with respect to all that can be deemed essential; for there is no sect of Christians who do not believe that Christ was sent of God; that he is the true Messiah; that he worked miracles, and suffered and died and rose again from the dead as related in the four Gospels; that after his resurrection he ascended to heaven and became possessed of universal dominion, being made head over all things in this world; and that he will hereafter make a second appearance on

this

this earth, and come from heaven to raise all mankind from death, to judge the world in righteousness, to bestow eternal life on the truly virtuous, and to punish the workers of iniquity.

These are the grand facts of Christianity, which *Calvinists* and *Arminians*, *Trinitarians* and *Unitarians*, *Papists* and *Protestants*, *Churchmen* and *Dissenters* all equally believe. More especially; with respect to the purpose of Christ's mission, we all equally hold that he came to call sinners to repentance, to teach us the knowledge of God and our duty, to save us from sin and death, and to publish a covenant of grace by which all sincere penitents and good men are assured of favour and complete happiness in his future everlasting kingdom.

But to bring all nearer to a point.

The information which most properly constitutes the Gospel does not consist of many particulars. It may be reduced to *one* proposition. The word GOSPEL, I have

I have said, signifies GOOD NEWS; or (as the New Testament calls it) *glad tidings of great joy to all people.* And the New-Testament when it thus describes the Gospel has one particular information in view. An information which is indeed completely joyful. I mean, the future coming of Christ to destroy death, and to reinstate us in a happy immortality; or, in other words, the glad tidings of pardon to penitents, and a resurrection from death to *eternal life through Jesus Christ.* It is impossible there should be any information so important as this; and all Christians believe it; and maintain that the truth of it has been demonstrated by signs and miracles, and, particularly, by the resurrection of Christ, and his consequent ascension and exaltation. This information includes all that we have any reason to be anxious about; and we should regard with indifference all disputes that leave us in possession of it; and there are no disputes

disputes among those who take the *New Testament* for a rule of faith which do *not* leave us in possession of it. A deliverance from death, through the power of Christ, to be judged according to our works; and, if virtuous, to enter upon a new and happy life which shall never end: This is the sum and substance of the Gospel; and, also, the sum and substance of all that should interest human beings. The evidence for it which the Gospel gives removes all doubts about it; and is sufficient, whether we believe any thing else or not, to carry us (if virtuous) with triumph through this world. What then signify the differences among Christians about other points? Or of what consequence is it that they have different ways of explaining this point itself? Give me but the fact that Christ is the *resurrection* and the *life*, and explain it as you will. Give me but this single truth, that ETERNAL LIFE *is the gift of God through Jesus Christ our Lord and Saviour*, and I shall be be perfectly easy with respect to the contrary opinions which are entertained about the dignity of Christ; about his nature, person, and offices; and the *manner* in which he saves us. Call him, if you please, simply a *man* endowed with extraordinary powers; or call him a super-angelic being who appeared in human nature for the purpose of accomplishing our salvation; or say (if you can admit a thought so shockingly absurd) that it was the second of three co-equal persons in the Godhead forming one person with a human soul that came down from heaven and suffered and died on the cross: Say that he saves us merely by being a messenger from God to reveal to us eternal life and to confer it upon us; or say, on the contrary, that he not only *reveals* to us eternal life and confers it upon us, but has *obtained* it for us by offering himself a propitiatory sacrifice on the cross, and making satisfaction to the justice of the Deity for our sins: I shall think such dif-

differences of litle moment provided the fact is allowed, that Chrift did rife from the dead and will raife *us* from the dead; and that all righteous penitents will, through God's grace in him, be accepted and made happy for ever.

In order to affift you in forming a juft idea of the nature of the differences among Chriftians, I will dwell a little on fome of them.

The chief of thefe differences have been thofe which I have juft recited with refpect to the perfon and offices of Chrift, fome maintaining his fimple humanity; others his fuperiority to man and pre-exiftence; and others his fupreme divinity. And, again, fome maintaining that he faves us only by his inftruction and example, and government: and others, that he faves us by being the procuring caufe of our falvation, and paying down an equivalent for it. Is it not obvious with refpect to thefe differences,
that

that they affect not the doctrine itself of our salvation by Christ; and that however they are determined, the foundation of our hopes remains the same? I will endeavour to illustrate this by putting a similar case.

Suppose a man to have lost a rich inheritance, and to be languishing under a distemper which will soon cut him off for ever from this world. Suppose, in these circumstances, a benefactor to appear, who brings with him, at the expence of much trouble, a remedy for the distemper and administers it to him, saves his life, and at the same time restores him to his inheritance, and to riches, splendour, and happiness. Would he, in this case, be very anxious about determining whether his benefactor was a *native* or a *foreigner*, a *private man* or a *prince?* Or whether the toil which he had gone through to save him was derived from his own spontaneous benevolence, or from an instrumentality to which he had submitted in order

order to convey the benevolence of another? Though such enquiries might engage his curiosity, would he reckon them of great importance to his interest? would he not, whatever the true answer to them was, have equal reason to rejoice in the service done him, and to be thankful for it?

Another subject of dispute among Christians has been the origin of that state of sin and mortality in which we find ourselves, and which gave occasion to the coming of the Messiah. All agree in deriving it from an event called the FALL of man, which happened at the commencement of this world. But very opposite accounts are given by divines of the nature and consequences of this FALL; some taking the history of it in Genesis in the strictly literal sense, and maintaining the doctrine of the imputation of Adam's sin to all his posterity; and others denying this doctrine, and believing the account of the

fall

fall to be in a great measure allegorical. But, in reality, it does not much signify whether we are able or not to satisfy ourselves on these points. This is of no more importance in this case than it would be in the case just mentioned, that a person dying of a distemper should be able to account for it, and to trace the events which brought it upon him. We find ourselves frail, degenerate, guilty, and mortal beings. The causes under the Divine government which brought us into this state lie far out of our sight; and, perhaps, were a naked representation of them made to us we should be only perplexed and confounded. It is enough to know that a Deliverer has been provided for us, who has shed his blood for the remission of his sins, and conquered death for every man by submitting to it himself. Instead of quarrelling about *Adam*'s fall, and losing our time and our tempers in litigations about original sin imputed and inherent, we should learn to take our state as we find it, and to employ ourselves earnestly about nothing but securing that better state, that glorious immortality, to the assured hope of which we have been raised by the redemption that is in Christ.

I will further instance in the disputes about justification. There are no disputes which have disturbed the Christian church much more; nor are there any which can appear to a considerate man more unmeaning and trifling. The principal subject of these disputes has been the question, whether we are justified by faith alone, or by faith in conjunction with good works. You should consider, with respect to this question, that those who hold notions the most rigid make justifying faith to be the seed and principle of personal holiness; and that there is no sect of Christians (however extravagant their doctrines may be) which has not *some expedient* or *salvo* for maintaining the necefnecessity of good works. If they say that personal holiness is not a *condition* of justification, they say what amounts to the same, that it is a *qualification* which must be found in all justified persons, and that without it we cannot be accepted. If they say that we are justified by faith alone, they add, that we cannot be justified by that faith which is alone (that is, by a faith not accompanied with good works) and that it is only on the virtuous believer, or the man who proves the truth of his faith by his works, that the grace of God in Christ will confer future happiness. How trifling then have been the controversies on this subject? As long as all acknowledge that it is only that faith which works by love, which purifies the heart and reforms the conduct, that can justify us; of what consequence is it to determine the particular manner in which it justifies us? As long as all hold that the practice of righteousness is necessary to bring us to heaven, what does it signify whether it is neceſſary as the *condition* of heaven, or as an indiſpenſible *qualification* for it?

Farther. There have been violent diſputes about the future reſurrection of mankind; ſome maintaining that the very body which had been laid in the grave (and afterwards made a part, perhaps, of a million of other bodies) is to be raiſed up; and others denying this, and aſſerting more rationally, that the doctrine of the reſurrection relates more to the *man* than to the *body*, and means only our *reviviſcence* after the incapacitation of death, or our becoming again embodied and living ſpirits in a new ſtate of exiſtence, it being, in their opinion, a circumſtance of no conſequence (provided the living *agent* is the ſame) whether the *body* is the ſame or not. In truth, it ſeems very plain, that our preſent and our future bodies muſt be eſſentially different. The one is *fleſh and blood.* The other is not te be *fleſh and*

and blood; for St. Paul tells us expressly, that *flesh and blood cannot inherit the kingdom of God.* But be this as it will; the dispute on this subject is of no particular consequence. Provided we know that we are to be raised up, we need not be very anxious to know *with what bodies we are to be raised up.* There is no more reason for disturbing ourselves about this, than there would be (were we going to take possession of an inheritance) to disturb ourselves about the materials of the dress in which we shall enter upon it.

Akin to this subject of dispute is another which has much perplexed the minds of many good Christians, and about which they have given way to many very unreasonable prejudices. I shall hope that those who now hear me are superior to these prejudices; and, therefore, I will be explicit on this subject. The subject I mean, is " the intermediate state between " death and the resurrection." The common persuasion is, that this intermediate state is to be a state of rewards and punishments.

nifhments. But many think the fcripture account to be, that rewards and punifhments are not to begin till the general judgment; and, confequently, that a fufpenfion of all our powers takes place at death which will continue till the morning of the refurrection, when the wicked fhall awake to everlafting fhame and contempt, but the righteous to life eternal. The obfervation I have made on the other fubjects of difpute which I have mentioned, is particularly applicable to this. It is a difpute about the manner and circumftances of a fcripture doctrine and not about the doctrine itfelf. Let the fact be acknowledged (as it is by every Chriftian) that we are to be raifed up from death; and, if virtuous, to live for ever in a better ftate through the grace of God in Chrift: Let, I fay, this fact be acknowledged, and we need not care fhould the truth be that it is to be preceded by a ftate of fleep and infenfibility. On this fuppofition, death will only be rendered more awful; for when the exercife of our mental

tal powers ceafes, the flux of time ceafes with it; the lapfe of ages becomes no more than the tick of a watch, or the vibratian of a pendulum; and, were we *never* to be recovered, *eternity* itfelf would be nothing to us. Whether, therefore, there is an intermediate ftate or not, death will to every man be the fame with an *immediate* entrance on another world, and that which many of our brethren are anxious about will happen. This is evident if there *is* an intermediate ftate: And if there is *not*, it is equally evident; becaufe, in this cafe, the moment of death will appear to be the moment of our refurrection though myriads of ages may have intervened, and clofing our eyes on this world will be opening them on the day of retribution, and feeing Chrift coming to judge mankind, and to be admired in all the virtuous and faithful. And, let me here afk, is not this a more pleafing profpect to good men, and a more dreadful one to wicked men, than the profpect of a long interval of delay and expectation in an intermediate state? Were you now going to embark for a voyage, would it be difagreeable to you to think that, whatever seas may intervene, the moment of your taking sail would to you be the very same with the moment of your landing on the shore of a better country? Or, were you now stepping into a bed after a fatiguing day, would it be disagreeable to you to know that a deep sleep will seize you, lock up all your powers, annihilate the night to you, and join the time of your lying down to the time of your getting up fresh and happy the next morning? I do not, however, mean to say, that I believe this will be actually the case. There are texts of scripture which I cannot easily reconcile to it. God only knows what the truth is in this instance. I only mean to say, that the difference of opinion about it should give us no trouble. In a little time our doubts will be resolved, and death itself,

itself, that great teacher, will inform and satisfy us.

But it is time to come to a conclusion.

The use we should make of what I have been saying, is to learn tranquillity and charity amidst the jarring opinions which prevail in the Christian church. None of them, you have heard, extend to fundamentals. In truth, there is but one thing fundamental, and that is, " an honest " mind." But by fundamentals I mean the doctrines which are most properly the fundamentals of the Christian religion, and constitute the information which it was intented to communicate to us. He that runs may read these doctrines in the *New Testament*; and it is not possible to mistake them. Extremes the most distant, I have shewn you, agree in them, and leave us every thing that is essential to our support and comfort in passing through the world. Pardon to *sinful* men; and a resurrection to *dying* men are all that nearly ly concern us. These, according to all opinions, are assured to us by the Gospel; and they make it, indeed, what my text calls it, a GLORIOUS Gospel. *Glory be to God in the highest. On earth peace; and good-will towards men.* Let us then love one another, and embrace with affection our fellow-christians of all persuasions, making allowances for their mistakes and prejudices. Many of them will indeed look upon *us* with aversion, and judge hardly of us, if we do not receive their schemes of Christianity, and worship God as they do. But let us shew our superior wisdom and candour by not judging hardly of *them*.

I shall, in my *next* discourses, give you an account of these schemes of Christianity. In *this* discourse my intention has been to prepare you for this account, by inculcating this truth; that however great the differences among Christians are, and however unreasonable many of their creeds may be, yet we are all agreed

in

in what is moſt important; and, particularly, in believing that Chriſt has *aboliſhed death, and brought life and immortality to light; and that, through the grace of God, he will be the author of eternal ſalvation to all that obey him.*

SERMON II.

OF THE CHRISTIAN DOCTRINE AS HELD BY TRINITARIANS AND CALVINISTS.

1 TIM. i. 11.

The glorious gospel of the blessed God.

THE most important of all enquiries are those which relate to the being, perfections, and providence of God. Next to these in importance are the enquiries, whether there is sufficient evidence for the truth of the Gospel; and if there is, what instruction it communicates? In my last discourse I entered on the discussion of the last of these questions, and endeavoured to shew you, that amidst all their differences,

ences, Christians are sufficiently agreed with respect to those essentials of the Gospel which make it, indeed, what the word *Gospel* imports, glad tidings and a glorious Gospel. According to all schemes, it is a dispensation of mercy to *sinful mortals*, conveying to them, through the ministry, death, and exaltation of Christ, the knowledge of God and their duty, pardon and favour, a resurrection from death, and a happy immortality. All accounts of Christianity agree, that it not only *reveals* and *announces* these inestimable benefits, but *ascertains* them by facts; and that Jesus Christ is the way, the truth, and the life, the conqueror of death, the future judge of mankind, and the author of eternal salvation to all that obey him. This, I have thought, a topic very necessary to be insisted upon and explained before I proceed to what I farther propose, which is, to give you some account of the different schemes of Christianity, and of that scheme in particular which I think
nearest

neareſt the truth. While, therefore, I ſhall be giving you ſuch an account, I wiſh you to recollect what I have ſaid on this topic, and to carry along with you the reflection, that there is no ſcheme of Chriſtianity received among its profeſſors which contradicts the only doctrine about which we have reaſon to be very anxious; I mean, " the doctrine of ſalvation and " eternal life by Jeſus Chriſt."

Were a well-authenticated *deed* brought to you which gave you a title to a good eſtate, would you (while its general deſign and purport were acknowledged) be very ſolicitous about the deciſion of any diſputes relating to the cauſes to which you owed the *deed*, the meaning of particular clauſes in it, or the character and rank of the friend by whoſe inſtrumentality you had received it. The Goſpel is our title to immortality: It contains that covenant of grace which ſecures it to us; and Chriſt is the friend by whoſe inſtrumentality it has been declared and confirmed,

firmed, and will be bestowed upon us. While agreed thus far, let us not suffer ourselves to indulge impatience or resentment when we hear some saying that Christ was a mere *man*, others that he was a super-angelic *being*, and others that he was *God* himself in union with a *man*; or when we are told by one party that he died to make satisfaction to Divine justice for the sins of the world, and by another party that he died only to bear testimony to the truth, to prove and confirm the forgiving mercy of God, and to acquire the power of conferring upon us the blessings of the covenant of grace.

But, though I would thus caution you against being shocked by the opposite opinions which are entertained among Christians, and prepare you for hearing, without being disturbed, the account I shall give of them; I do not mean to intimate that it is of *no* consequence how we think about the points disputed among
Chris-

Christians. Though, for the reasons I have given, this is not of *such* consequence as to justify that distress which some good men feel when they hear of opinions of the Gospel contrary to their own; yet it is without doubt the duty of every one, as far as he has abilities and opportunities, to endeavour to think rightly about these disputed points, and by careful and impartial enquiry to avoid gross errors. The better we are informed about the controversies among Christians, and the more correct our judgements, the more respectable we shall be, and also the more useful and valuable members of the Christian church; provided we take care to add to our knowledge brotherly kindness, and suppress in ourselves every tendency to intolerance and uncharitableness.

I have, therefore, thought that, after shewing you how far we are all *agreed* in our conceptions of the Gospel, it would not

not be improper to shew you how far Christians *differ*, and to give a brief representation of the principal schemes of Christianity which they have adopted. In executing this design, I shall give an account of only *three schemes*, because they are the principal, and all other schemes may be ranged under one or other of them. Of these three schemes, two form *extremes*; and one a *middle* scheme. I shall begin with giving you an account of the two extremes, after which I shall make some observations on them, and then proceed to an account of that *middle* scheme, which I think the true one, and which I shall endeavour to support by some arguments.

The first of the two extremes just mentioned has been distinguished under the names of *Athanasianism* and *Calvinism*; and the other under the name of *Socinianism*. One of these carries our notions very high of Christianity; and the other sinks them very low. The differences between them respect four points.

First.

First. The nature of the Deity.

Secondly. The nature and consequences of that fall of man which brought us into our present state.

Thirdly. The nature and dignity of Christ.

And Fourthly. The nature of that interposition of Christ by which he is the Saviour of the world.

I shall first mention to you the chief particulars in the *Athanasian* and *Calvinistic* scheme, as far as it respects these four points.

With respect to the SUPREME DEITY, this scheme makes him to consist of *three persons the same in substance, and equal in power and glory.* The first of these three persons, and the fountain of Divinity to the other two, it makes to be the FATHER. The *second* person is called the SON; and said to be derived from the Father by an eternal generation of an ineffable and incomprehensible nature in the essence

essence of the GODHEAD. The *third* person is the HOLY GHOST, derived from the Father and the Son; but not by generation as the Son is derived from the Father, but by an eternal and incomprehensible PROCESSION. Each of these persons are (according to this scheme) very and eternal God as much as the Father himself; and yet, though distinguished in the manner I have said, they do not make *three Gods* but *one God* [a].

[a] " In the unity of the Godhead there be *three per-*
" *sons* of one substance, power, and eternity; the
" Father, the Son, and the Holy Ghost. The Son
" begotten from everlasting of the Father, very and
" eternal God, of one substance with the Father.
" The Holy Ghost *proceeding* from the Father and
" the Son, of one substance, majesty, and glory with
" the Father and the Son, very and eternal God."
First, Second, and Fifth Articles of the Church of England.
" God the Father of Heaven; God the Son, Re-
" deemer of the world; God the Holy Ghost pro-
" ceeding from the Father and the Son; Holy, Bles-
" sed,

With respect to the FALL OF MAN, this scheme maintains the doctrine of original sin *imputed* and *inherent*, whereby every person born into this world deserves, before he has contracted *actual* guilt, God's

"sed, and Glorious Trinity, three persons and one
"God: Have mercy upon us." *Litany.*

"The Father is made of none; neither created
"nor begotten. The Son is of the Father alone;
"not made, or created, but begotten. The Holy
"Ghost is of the Father and the Son; neither made,
"nor created, nor begotten, but proceeding."

"There are three persons in the Godhead, the
"Father, the Son, and the Holy Ghost; and these
"three are one God, the same in substance, and equal
"in power and glory." *Question Sixth in the Shorter Catechism of the Reverend Assembly of Divines.*

"I believe, first, in God the Father, who *made*
"*me* and all the world. Secondly, in God the Son,
"who hath *redeemed* me and all mankind. Thirdly,
"in God the Holy Ghost, who *sanctifieth* me and all
"the elect people of God. *Church Catechism.*

Divines have laboured to shew, that believing in these three Gods is consistent with believing in but *one* God. But what a riddle must this appear to a child?

God's wrath and future damnation. By original sin *imputed* is meant the *imputation* of *Adam*'s sin to all his posterity: And by original sin *inherent* is meant that fault and corruption of the nature of man whereby he is rendered prone to all evil, and so averse to all good as not to have the power of doing any thing acceptable to God, or, by his own natural strength, of turning to God, or even preparing himself for calling upon God[b]. In short, this

---

[b] " Original sin is the fault and corruption of the nature of every man engendered of the offspring of Adam, whereby he is very far gone from original righteousness, and of his own nature inclined to evil; and, therefore, in every person born into this world it deserves God's wrath and damnation." *Ninth Article of the Church of England.* " The condition of man after the fall of Adam is such, that he cannot turn or prepare himself by his own natural strength and good works to faith and calling upon God." *Tenth Article.* " Being by nature born in sin and children of wrath, we are by baptism made the children of grace." *Church Catechism.*

this part of this scheme cannot be better expressed than it is in that catechism which has been received as the standard of orthodox divinity among Protestant Dissenters, and which many of our good brethren still hold in high veneration. The words of this Catechism are " That " all mankind fell in Adam and were " brought by his transgression into a state " of *sin* and of *misery*; that the *sinfulness* " of this state consists in the guilt of " Adam's sin, the want of original righ- " teousness, and the corruption of our " whole nature; and that the *misery* of " this state consists in the loss of com- " munion with God, and in being under " his wrath and curse, and liable to all " the miseries of this life, and to the " pains of hell for ever^c."

With

---

^c Assembly's Catechism, Questions 16th, 17th, 18th, and 19th. " The fall brought upon mankind " the loss of communion with God, and his dis- " pleasure and curse; so that we are BY NATURE chil- " dren

With respect to the THIRD great point, or the nature and dignity of Christ, this scheme teaches us that he consists of *two* natures; by one of which he is simply a *man*; and by the other, the second person in the TRINITY, of one substance with the Father, begotten from everlasting, and very and eternal God [d]. These two natures are, according

"dren of wrath, bond-slaves to Satan, and justly liable to all punishments in this world and in that which is to come. And the punishments in the world to come are separation from God, and *most grievous torments in soul and body without intermission in hell-fire for ever.*" Assembly's Larger Catechism. "Man by the fall hath wholly lost all ability of will to any spiritual good; so that a natural man, being dead in sin, is not able to convert himself, or to *prepare* himself for conversion." *Scotch Confession of Faith*, chap. 9th.

[d] "The Son, of one substance with the Father, took man's nature, so that two whole and perfect natures, the Godhead and manhood, were joined together in one person, making one Christ, very God and very man, who truly suffered, was crucified,

cording to this scheme, whole and perfect natures distinct from one another, but joined together in *one person* making one Christ, very God, and, at the same time, very man. In the catechism just quoted this is expressed in the following words. " The Redeemer of God's elect " is the Lord Jesus Christ, who being the " eternal Son of God became man, and " so

" cified, dead, and buried, to reconcile his Father " to us, and to be a sacrifice, not only for original " guilt, but also for the actual sins of men." *Second Article of the Church of England.* " The right " faith is, that we believe that Jesus Christ is God " and man; perfect God and perfect man; and yet " that he is not *two*, but *one*; one, by taking the " manhood into God, and unity of *person*." *Athanasian Creed.*

" I believe in our Lord Jesus Christ, begotten of " his Father before all worlds; God of God, light " of light, very God of very God; *begotten*, not " *made*, being of one substance with the Father, by " whom all things were made; who, for us men " and our salvation, came down from heaven and " was incarnate of the Virgin Mary, &c." *Nicene Creed.*

" so was and continues to be God and
" man in two distinct natures, and one
" person, for ever[c]." I will here only add, that this union of *two natures* in Christ so as to make *one person*, has been called by a very peculiar name, in order to distinguish it from the union of *three persons* making *one nature* in the Deity. It has been called, the HYPOSTATICAL UNION.

The FOURTH great point about which I have said that Christians differ, is the nature of that interposition of Christ by which he is the Saviour of the world. The scheme I am describing makes it to consist in a translation of the guilt of sinners from them to Christ, and his substituting himself for them, and undergoing in his own person the punishment due to them, and thus purchasing their salvation by making satisfaction to God's justice, and offering an equivalent for it.

[c] Assembly's Catechism. 21st. Question.

it. But this is a part of this scheme so important, that it will be proper to trace it a little higher and to give a more explicit representation of it.

One of its leading doctrines is, the doctrine of absolute and unconditional predestination. According to this doctrine, God has for his own glory (as our catechism tells us [f]) fore-ordained *whatever* comes to pass; and, in particular, appointed a part of the fallen race of man to everlasting happiness, but left the greatest part to perish and to sink without remedy into everlasting misery. In order to bring about the salvation of the elected part, a covenant of redemption was entered into before the world began, between the three persons in the TRINITY (the Father, the Son, and the Holy Ghost) by which the second person engaged to make satisfaction to the Godhead, and to offer on the cross a *propitiatory sacrifice* in order to expiate the

[f] Question 7th.

the offences of the *elect*, and to obtain for them the benefits of effectual calling, justification, sanctification, adoption, and future eternal glory. In pursuance of this compact, the second person in the Trinity came down from heaven, entered the Virgin's womb, and suffered and died to fulfil (as the Articles of the Church of England say) " the everlasting purpose of
" God whereby, before the foundations
" of the world were laid, he had decreed
" by his counsel to deliver from curse and
" damnation those whom he had *chosen*
" in Christ out of mankind; and to bring
" them, by Christ, to everlasting salvati-
" on as vessels made for honour." Wherefore (as the same Articles declare) they are called in time, justified freely by God's grace, sanctified by his spirit, made his sons by adoption, walk religiously in all good works, and at length attain to everlasting felicity [s].

THIS

---

[s] Article 17th.

This is a brief recital of that system of Christian faith which has been generally called *Calvinism*: And you may observe, that it includes in it (besides the doctrines of three co-ordinate persons in the Godhead forming *one* nature, and of *two natures* in Jesus Christ forming *one* person) the five following doctrines.

First, The doctrine of absolute predestination and election.

Secondly, The doctrine of original sin.

Thirdly, The doctrine of the total impotence of man and irresistible grace, in opposition to free-will.

Fourthly, The doctrine of *particular* in opposition to *universal* redemption.

And Fifthly, The doctrine of the perseverance of saints after being once called and converted.

These *five* doctrines have been called, by way of distinction and eminence, the FIVE POINTS. They are the points about which the sect called *Arminians* differ from *Calvinists*: And, in litigating them, volumes

lumes without number have been written, much zeal employed, and an infinity of what is moſt important in religion (I mean, charity and a good temper) has been loſt. But there is one *other* point connected with thoſe now ſpecified, which forms an eſſential part of this ſyſtem; and which, in juſtice to it, ought to be mentioned. That is; the doctrine of juſtification by faith alone, and the imputed righteouſneſs of Chriſt. All the orthodox confeſſions of faith agree in declaring that we are accounted righteous before God, not for our good works, but only for the merit of Chriſt. And this doctrine our Church Articles declare to be a moſt wholeſome doctrine[h]. And ſo
im-

---

[h] "We are accounted righteous before God only for the merit of our Lord and Saviour Jeſus Chriſt, by faith; and not for our own good works or deſervings. Wherefore that we are juſtified by faith only is a moſt wholeſome doctrine, and very full of comfort as more largely is expreſſed in the homi-
ly

important has it been held, that it has been called the doctrine by which, as it is received or rejected, the church of Christ must stand or fall[1]. You should remember, however, that those who maintain this doctrine do not mean that we may be justified *without* good works. For, though they say that our good works cannot recommend us to God, and that " when done before the grace of Christ " they have even the nature of *sin*;" yet they at the same time say, that they are necessary as fruits of a true and living faith[k]; and, by a very nice distinction noticed

"ly of justification." *Article* 11th. "Justification is an act of God's free grace wherein he pardoneth all our sins, and accepteth us as righteous in his sight only for the righteousness of Christ imputed to us, and received by faith alone." *Assembly's Catechism Quest.* 33.

[1] *Articulus Stantis aut cadentis Ecclesiæ.*

[k] "Works done before the grace of Christ and the "inspiration of his spirit are not pleasant to God, "forasmuch as they spring not of faith in Christ. "Yea rather, we doubt not but they have the na- "ture

noticed in my last discourse, they assert, "that it is indeed faith *alone* that justifies "us, but not that faith which is alone[1]."

But I will proceed no farther in this recital lest I should lead you too far into the labyrinth of church divinity. What I have said is sufficient to give you a just idea of the first of the two extremes in the systems of faith adopted by Christians which I have proposed to state. I should now proceed to state that scheme of Christian faith which makes the other extreme. But chusing to reserve this for the next discourse, I will now conclude with a few observations on the scheme just described.

I fancy

"ture of sin." *Thirteenth Article of the Church of England.* "Albeit that good works which are the "fruits of faith and *follow justification* cannot put "away our sins; yet are they pleasing to God in "Christ, and spring necessarily out of a true and "lively faith," &c. *Article* 14th.

[1] *Fides sola justificat sed non fides quæ sola est.*

I fancy that by some parts of it your *good sense* as well as your feelings of benevolence must be shocked. Many enquiries concerning it will, upon the least reflection, offer themselves to you which cannot be easily answered. You may ask how we can be justified *freely* by the grace of God if a full *equivalent* has been paid for our redemption? How it is possible that God should make satisfaction to *himself* for the sins of the world? And how, if *three persons* acting different parts and sustaining different characters are each of them equally God, there can be but *one God?* Or, if this is possible, and *three persons* make but *one nature*, how it can[a] be possible

---

[a] Such it seems (in the opinion of *Trinitarians*) is this union of the divine and human nature in Christ, while yet the individuality of each is preserved, that it makes all that is true of the one equally true of the other. If this cannot be imagined, it must be impossible for an attentive person to join in one part of our established worship without shuddering. I mean, that

sible that *two natures* should make but *one person* in Jesus Christ?—You might farther ask, how a sin committed at the creation can be imputed to those who did not commit it, so as to subject them to wrath and punishment? How, in particular, this can be true of innocent babes of whom Christ says, that of such is the kingdom of heaven? How, if by denying to the greatest part of mankind the means of salvation, he has devoted them to eternal misery, he can be a just and a benevolent being? And why, if we have not free-will and can *do* nothing, it does not follow that we have " NOTHING TO DO?"

These and numberless other questions may be asked concerning the doctrines taught by this system; and it seems indeed to be, in most parts of it, a system

---

that part of the Litany which supplicates the mercy of God—by his holy nativity and circumcision—by his fastings and temptations—by his agony and bloody sweat—by his precious death and burial.

inconsistent with reason, injurious to the character of the ever-blessed Deity, and in the highest degree comfortless and discouraging. I will add, that it seems to me no less contrary to *scripture* than to *reason*; and I will just mention to you two instances of this.

The scriptures tell us that Christ died for *all*; that he was made lower than the angels for a little time to taste death for *every* man; and that he is the propitiation, not of the sins of Christians only, but for the sins of the whole world. But the advocates of this scheme tell us the contrary; that Christ died only for the *elect*, and that his dying for *all* means only his dying for *some* men of all ranks and conditions.—In like manner; the scriptures tell us that the one living and true God is God the Father of whom are all things, and who sent Christ into the world. *This is life eternal*, says our Saviour himself, *to know thee the only true God, and Jesus Christ whom thou hast sent.*
There

There are gods many, says St. Paul, *and there are lords many, but to* us *there is but one God the Father of whom are all things; and one Lord Jesus through whom are all things.* I need not point out to you the repugnancy between such declarations and some parts of the system I have represented. In truth, were any man (supposed unacquainted with the controversies which have arisen among Christians) to set himself to invent a system of faith so irrational and unscriptural as to be incapable of being received by Christians, he could scarcely think of one concerning which he would be more ready to form such a judgment. And yet—Oh! miserable imperfection of human beings—it is the system of christian divinity which has been for many ages generally received in the Christian church. It is the system which formerly all our ᵐ chil-

---

ᵐ In the Church Catechism it is taught children with the addition of a doctrine very like to *transub-*
stan-

dren were made to imbibe with their mother's milk, and to confider as moſt ſacred. It is the ſyſtem inculcated in all eſtabliſhed formularies of faith; and, particularly, in thoſe of England, Ireland, and Scotland. And, what is worſt of all, it is the ſyſtem to which the eſtabliſhed clergy in *Britain* and *Ireland* declare their aſſent on entering their office as public teachers, and without believing the very abſurdeſt part of which, one particular creed pronounces that we cannot be ſaved [n].

I muſt, however, obſerve to you, that this ſyſtem is held by different divines with very different degrees of ſtrictneſs, ſome carrying it much higher than others

For

ſtantiation; for it is ſcarcely poſſible a child ſhould have any other meaning when he is made to ſay, " that " the body and blood of Chriſt are *verily and indeed* " taken and received in the Lord's ſupper."

[n] In *Scotland*, if I am not miſtaken, the clergy are required not only to declare their belief of this ſyſtem, but that they will " conſtantly adhere to it," that is, never grow wiſer.

For inſtance. Some divines have thought the three perſons in the trinity only three different *characters* under which the ſupreme Deity acts; or three different *attributes* of his nature; while others have maintained that they are three different beings united by a common conſciouſneſs.

In the doctrine of *predeſtination* ſome include *reprobation* as well as *election*; while others make *reprobation* to be only *perterition:* That is, not an *appointment* to damnation, but an *abandonment* of all the non-elected poſterity of Adam by which they are left neceſſarily to periſh.

According to ſome, the eternal decree of predeſtination reſpected men as *fallen* beings; and this claſs of divines have been diſtinguiſhed under the name of *ſub*-lapſarians. But according to other divines (called *ſupra*-lapſarians) predeſtination was an arbitrary decree which reſpected men merely as *creatures*, and by which God, from his ſovereign good pleaſure only,

only, without any consideration of Adam's fall, made some of his posterity to be vessels of honour, and the rest to be vessels of wrath and misery, just as a potter from his good pleasure forms different portions of the same clay for noble or ignoble purposes.

Again; with respect to those consequences of the fall in which that half of mankind who die in infancy and between infancy and maturity are involved; some divines have maintained that, in consequence of the imputation of Adam's transgression, the taint of original sin, and the loss of original righteousness, they are so depraved and polluted, as to be the objects of God's vindictive justice and subject to the *pains of hell for ever*[n]: While others of a milder stamp have only maintained

---

[n] "ALL mankind by the fall have lost communion with God, are under his wrath and curse, and so made liable to all the miseries of this life, and to the pains of hell for ever." *Assembly's Catechism*, Question 19th.

tained that, if defcended from wicked parents, they will be *annihilated*; and that, if the offspring of righteous parents, they will be happy. This was the opinion of that eminent man and excellent poet to whom moſt of the congregations of Proteſtant Diſſenters are indebted for the Pſalms and Hymns they conſtantly uſe in public worſhip.

But I muſt reſtrain myſelf. I feel that I am in danger of tiring and perplexing you. I will, therefore, only add the following reflections.

Firſt, How pernicious are the effects of civil eſtabliſhments of religion? That ſyſtem of faith which I have deſcribed, and againſt which your *feelings* as well as your *reaſon* muſt revolt, is upheld by all the church eſtabliſhments in Chriſtendom, and the reception of it enforced by pains and penalties. This is true of even this land of diſtinguiſhed light and liberty. An act of *Queen Elizabeth* ſtill in force inflicts on all who ſpeak in derogation,

gation of the Book of Common Prayer fines for the firſt and ſecond offence; forfeiture of goods for the third; and impriſonment for life for the fourth offence. And an act of *King William* enacts, that " every perſon educated in the
" Chriſtian religion denying by writing,
" printing, teaching, or ſpeaking, any
" one of the three perſons in the Holy
" Trinity to be God, or maintaining that
" there are more Gods than one, ſhall,
" for the firſt offence, be rendered incap-
" able of holding any office; and, for the
" ſecond offence, be rendered incapable of
" bringing any action, or buying any
" lands, and ſuffer three years impriſon-
" ment." By ſpeaking, therefore, to you in the manner I have now done, I ſhould, at the time theſe acts paſſed, have expoſed myſelf to great danger. But, thanks be to God, the times in this country are happily altered. We can now think as we pleaſe, and profeſs

what

what we think: And, though the laws continue the same, we can rely on the generosity (not to say the justice) of the public for protection against them, while we keep within the limits of fair discussion and argument.—But I am wandering from the point I had in view.

I observed, that we may learn from what I have said the pernicious effects of civil establishments of religion. Had it not been for the support which the system I have described has derived from hence, it is scarcely conceivable that it could have stood its ground long in opposition to increasing light and knowledge. During the three first centuries from our Saviour's birth it was little known; nor did it gain a full settlement till civil power took Christianity under its patronage, and the grand apostacy foretold in the Scriptures begun in the Christian Church. Nothing, indeed, can be more horrible than the accounts in Ecclesiastical History of the

the furious controversies which the introduction of this system occasioned, and the torrents of blood which were shed before its principal articles came to be generally received. I refer to the disputes between *Athanasius* and *Arius* in the fourth century, which ended in the establishment of the present doctrine, " that Christ and the " Holy Spirit are *consubstantial* with the " Father."—The disputes between the *Nestorians* and their opponents, which ended in the establishment of the present doctrine of the *Hypostatical* union.—The disputes between St. *Austin* and the *Pelagians*, which ended in the establishment of the present doctrines of predestination and original sin.—And to the dispute, whether the Holy Ghost proceeded from the Father *only*, which ended in the establishment of the present doctrine, " that he " proceeds both from the Father and the " Son."

It is not possible to describe to you the convulsions into which these disputes

putes threw the Christian church in the fourth and fifth centuries; the *Anathemas* which the contending parties hurled against one another; and the dreadful rage with which the stronger party always harrassed the weaker party. I suppose I do not exaggerate when I say, that in these controversies millions of human sacrifices were offered at the shrine of religious bigotry. In truth; ecclesiastical history in general, and this part of it more especially, is little more than a history of the worst passions of the human heart worked up by ecclesiastical zeal into a diabolical virulence and madness. Christians have lately grown wiser, and, I hope, better. We can now look back with astonishment on those days of ignorance, and welcome the approach of that period when the Gospel shall be better understood, jargon give way to reason, and peace and tolerance prevail universally.

sally. This leads me to give you a necessary caution.

I have expressed pretty strongly my disapprobation of the system of Divinity which I have stated. But I would exhort you earnestly to avoid all uncharitableness with respect to those of our fellow-christians who still hold this system. In consequence of the spread of the principles of humanity, it is now held by its warmest advocates with milder dispositions than formerly; and though, in the last century and the beginning of this, they would probably have devoutly burnt me, yet now there are few of them in whose hands I would not trust myself, without the least apprehension of being at all injured in my person, property, or liberty. We have had lately, among Protestant Dissenters, a striking proof of this change of temper in our *Trinitarian* and *Calvinistical* brethren. Not long ago, as I have just intimated, it would have been

a point

a point of piety with them not to tolerate minifters who profefs, as moft of the *Prefbyterian* minifters now do, *Unitarian* principles. But had it been propofed to them to concur with *fuch* minifters in *feeking* a toleration, they would have been fhocked. This, however, has lately been the conduct of our *Trinitarian* brethren. They have joined with me and others in applications to parliament, which at laft proved fuccefsful, for granting the benefit of toleration to all Proteftant preachers of all denominations, reprobating all penal laws in religion, difdaining to afk a liberty for themfelves which would not be equally enjoyed by *Unitarians* and *Socinians*, and even declaring a preference, could it have been obtained, of a toleration which would have given legal protection to the worfhip of all peaceable men of all fects and religions. Nothing can do them greater honour.

Without all doubt, neither virtue nor good fenfe belongs exclufively to any one religious sect. We see continually that wise and worthy men fall into great mistakes, and are capable of receiving as sacred the grossest absurdities. But this is of little consequence; our acceptance with God depending on the sincerity of of our hearts and the faithfulness of our endeavours to find out truth, and not on the rectitude of our judgments. Many an *Athanasian* and *Calvinist* will hereafter rejoice in heaven with many of those *Unitarians* and *Arminians* whom now, from mistaken views, he consigns to hell°; and he

° By delivering this sentiment I have subjected myself to the *Anathema* in the 18th Article of the Church of *England*, which declares those " accursed who " presume to say that every man shall be saved by the " law or sect which he professes, if he be diligent to " frame his life according to that law and the light " of nature; holy Scripture setting out to us only " the name of Christ whereby men must be saved." It is strange that our rulers can continue the imposition of this article, the *Athanasian* Creed, &c. &c.

he will then be surprised at his own rashness. Let us, therefore, learn to respect one another amidst all our differences.

What is most to be lamented in the system I have stated, is its tendency to lead

The enemies of reformation do not sufficiently consider, that by opposing, in enlightened times, all attempts to remove such shocking blemishes from our established code of faith and worship, they expose the hierarchy to particular danger of a sudden and total overthrow. As a friend to the free progress of truth, and an enemy to all slavish hierarchies, I could almost wish they may persevere in their obstinacy.

I am sensible that the Article just quoted may be understood to signify no more than that virtuous Heathens, Jews, and Mahometans, will be saved only through Jesus Christ. But this could not be the meaning of the framers of these Articles. It is probable that no such Catholic idea ever entered their minds as the possibility of the salvation of virtuous men of *all* religions. Much less could they think that those Heretics might be *saved* in *another* world whom they thought it their duty to *burn* in *this* world; and concerning whom the nation in its public devotions is ordered to declare, that they will without doubt perish everlastingly.

The

lead those who embrace it to lay an undue stress upon it, and to think that all who reject it deny the Lord that bought them, and are enemies to God and

The decisions of the Reverend Assembly of Presbyterian Divines sitting at *Westminster*, are the same on these subjects with those of the church of *England*. " Good works, they say, done by unregenerate men, " since they proceed not from a heart purified by " faith, are sinful, and cannot please God, or make " a man meet to receive the grace of God; and yet " the neglect of them is *more* sinful and displeasing " to God." *Assembly's Confession of Faith*, chap. 16th Sect. 7th. " Infants and others, *if elected*, are " saved. But all not elected, though called by the " ministry of the word, never come to Christ, and, " therefore, cannot be saved; much less can men " not professing the Christian religion be saved in " any other way whatever, be they never so diligent " to frame their lives according to the light of na- " ture and the law of that religion they profess; and " to assert they may, is very pernicious and to be " detested." *Ib.* ch. 10, sect. 3 and 4. Concerning all who oppose such doctrines as these, and maintain opinions contrary to the known principles of Christianity, they say, " they may be
" law-

and Chrift. This contracts their benevolence, and difpofes them to view with difguft a confiderable part of their Chriftian brethren, it being fcarcely poffible they

"fully called to account and proceeded againft by
"the cenfures of the church and the power of the
"civil magiftrate; who has authority, and whofe
"duty it is to preferve unity in the church, to keep
"the truth of God pure and entire, and to fupprefs
"herefy." But at the fame time it is added, that,
in doing this, the civil magiftrate is to be only the
executioner of prefbyteries and fynods, "with whom
"he is to confult and advife, and to whom it be-
"longeth to decide controverfies of faith, and to fet
"down rules for the ordering of the public worfhip
"of God and government of his church, and *autho-*
"*ritatively* to determine the fame; which determina-
"tions are to be received, with reverence and fub-
"miffion, as coming from a power which is the or-
"dinance of God." *Ibid.* ch. 20. fect. 4. ch. 23.
fect. 3. and ch. 31. fect. 3. How adverfe to every
principle of religious liberty and charity are thefe decifions? Many in this affembly had fmarted feverely under the exercife of *prelatical* authority; and this fhould have led them to deteft fuch principles. But it appears from this Confeffion of
Faith

they should *love* those whom they think God *hates.* Such uncharitableness is miserable and frightful. Let us avoid it as much as we can. It will be more inexcusable in *us* than it is in *them,* in proportion to the degree in which our sen-

Faith and their subsequent conduct, that they wanted only to transfer the seat of church tyranny and the powers of persecution from the *bishops* to *themselves.* In justice, however, to their characters, it should be considered, that their narrowness and intolerance were the faults of the age in which they lived. They had not yet escaped far enough from the darkness of popery to enjoy the light and comfort of enlarged sentiments. Those venerable reformers, in particular, to whom we owe our present Church Service and the 39 Articles, were excellent men; and though, from a regard to what they thought to be *sacred* truth, they would burn *others*, they proved that, from the same principle, they would also burn *themselves.*—I must add, that this is an apology for them which renders their successors in the present times more inexcusable. The dark age is gone; and yet its errors and barbarities are continued to burden the consciences of good men, and to mislead and disgrace the national worship.

sentiments are more liberal. And in this lies one unspeakable advantage of liberal sentiments. They open our hearts to all about us, and communicate catholic dispositions. By connecting the favour of God with nothing but an honest mind, and causing us to think of him as a friend to every sincere enquirer, they leave room for the exercise of all the kind affections. They extirpate the wretched prejudices which make us shy of one another; and enable us to regard, with equal satisfaction and pleasure, our neighbours, friends, and acquaintance, be their modes of worship or their systems of faith what they will.

But I have detained you too long. What I am next to proceed to is an account of the scheme of Christianity which has been commonly called *Socinianism*, This shall be reserved for the next discourse.

SERMON III.

OF THE CHRISTIAN DOCTRINE AS HELD BY UNITARIANS ᵃ AND SOCINIANS.

---

1 TIM. i. 11.

The glorious gospel of the blessed God.

IN discoursing to you from these words I have proposed to give you an account of that Gospel here called by St. Paul *the glo-*

ᵃ By *Unitarians* I mean those Christians who believe there is but one God and one object of religious worship; and that this one God is the *Father* only, and not a Trinity consisting of Father, Son, and Holy Ghost. An *Unitarian*, therefore, may or may not be a believer in Christ's pre-existence; and it will *glorious Gospel of the blessed God.* In doing this I have proposed to shew you.

First, What those Articles of the Christian faith are about which all Christians are agreed. This was the subject of my first discourse; and, in speaking to you upon it, I endeavoured to shew you, that all Christians are agreed with respect to what is most important in the information given us by the Gospel—That the differences among them are chiefly different modes of explaining those fundamental facts which all equally believe.—And that, consequently, these differences afford no just reason for any alarm to those Christians who may be unacquainted with the disputes which have taken place in the Christian church. We all believe, I observed, that the glad tidings

---

will appear in the sequel, that those who deny this doctrine have, on this account, no more right to this appellation than those antient Heathens had, who, though they might believe in one Supreme Divinity, yet worshipped deified human spirits.

tidings which the Gospel brings are, *Peace on earth and good will towards men*, by the promise it makes of pardon and favour and a resurrection from death to an endless life, through that great Messiah who died and rose again. And this is all that can be interesting to us as guilty and mortal creatures.

I proceeded from hence to give you an account of the different schemes of the Gospel which have been adopted by Christians, after which I have proposed to give you an account of that scheme which, I think, the true scheme; and to endeavour to support it by some arguments.

I have divided the different schemes of Christianity into three; namely, the *Calvinists*, the *Socinian*, and a middle scheme between these two. I have already given a sufficient account of the first of these schemes; and I shall now give you a brief account of the *Socinian* scheme. These schemes form (as I observed in my former discourse) the two extremes into which

Christians have gone in their opinions of the Gospel. One carries our notions very high on the narrow side; and the other sinks them as low on the contrary side. Against this last scheme there are strong prejudices among many good Christians, and you will find that in two leading points I think it wrong: But that it maintains all that we need be anxious about in Christianity, and that consequently the prejudices against it have no just foundation, will probably appear from the following recital of its principal doctrines.

In order to go along with me here you should carry in your minds the FOUR heads under whch I have ranged the subjects of difference in the opinions of Christians. First, the nature of the Deity—Secondly, the nature and dignity of Christ—Thirdly, the fall of man and its consequences—And, Fourthly, the nature and effect of Christ's interposition.

First,

First, with respect to the nature of the Deity *Socinians* differ from *Trinitarians* and *Calvinists* in holding the doctrine of his UNITY with more strictness. In opposition to the doctrine of *three* persons making one God, they maintain that the essence of the Deity is simple and undivided; that God the Father only (and not the Father, the Son, and the Holy Ghost) is the true and living God, and the fountain of all power and perfection in the universe; and that to elevate any other beings to an equality with him is idolatry and impiety,

Secondly, With respect to the FALL, *Socinians* allow that there has been such an event, and that by it mankind have been brought lower in the scale of beings, and subjected to the imperfections of the present state and particularly to the evil of death [b]. But they reject the doctrine of the

[b] There are some who give such interpretations of the account in the 3d chap. of Genesis and the subsequent

the imputation of Adam's transgression to his posterity, and such a total corruption of our natures by original sin as deprives us of free-will, and subjects us before we have committed *actual* sin (and, therefore, even *infants*) to the displeasure of God and future punishment.

Thus far I go entirely with them, as do many other Christians who yet are by no means to be considered as holding the opinions which most properly form the *Socinian* system of Christianity. What distinguishes this system is the doctrine they maintain with respect to the two other subjects of difference which I have mentioned; or the dignity of Christ, and the sense in which he is our Saviour.

With quent references to it in the sacred writings (and particularly in Rom. the 5th chap. and 1 Cor. 15th chap.) as make them no evidence of any such event (introductory of death) as is commonly understood by the FALL. But these interpretations, and the opinion grounded upon them are so singular, that I have not thought them worth particular notice.

With respect to the dignity of Christ, they hold that he was simply a man; and, consequently, that he had no existence before his birth and appearance in this world; maintaining, however, at the same time, that by the extraordinary powers with which he was endowed, and a communication of the Spirit of God to him without measure, he was raised far above *common* men, and distinguished so much from them as to be infallible and impeccable [c], and capable of becoming, immediately after his resurrection, the Sovereign of angels and the Judge of mankind. They have in particular gone so far in their ideas of the *present* dignity of Christ, though a mere man, as to assert that he is exalted to a sovereignty over all creatures, and become a proper object of religious worship and adoration.

---

[c] Such was the *Socinian* doctrine formerly. It will appear in the next discourse that modern Socinians of the first character do not carry their ideas of Christ so high.

On this last point, however, they have been of different opinions: Many of them, (and particularly *Socinus*) maintaining zealously that Christ ought to be invoked and worshipped, while others of them scrupled this. And so miserable has been the disposition of religious men of all persuasions to intolerance, that even the Socinians formerly persecuted one another on account of this difference; and there is too much reason to believe that *Socinus* himself contributed to an imprisonment which occasioned the death of an amiable and worthy man among his followers who could not concur with him in this opinion [d].

At

---

[d] See Mr. *Toulman's Memoirs of the Life, Character, Sentiments, and Writings of Faustus Socinus*, p. 82, &c. See also Mr. *Lindsey's Historical view of the State of the Unitarian Doctrine and Worship*. A work which, while it gives the most humiliating view of the wretched blindness of many good men, manifests a candour in the author which does honour to his principles and character.

At present all that embrace *Socinianism* seem to be agreed (and, I think, very rightly) in condemning the doctrine as well as in reprobating the conduct of *Socinus* in this instance.

But, fourthly, with respect to the doctrine of our salvation by Jesus Christ, they hold that he is our Saviour by his example, by his instructions, and by that power to which he has been exalted to govern the Christian church, to raise mankind from death, and to bestow upon us the future reward of virtue. In other words; they make him a *Redeemer* and *Deliverer* not only as he was the greatest of all teachers and reformers; but, likewise as he has been made, in consequence of his sufferings and death, the *conveyer* of God's forgiving mercy and favour to mankind in a future happy eternity. They receive, therefore, in common with all other Christians, those great facts which are the foundation of
the

the Christian religion—the wonderful miracles of Christ by which he proved that the fullness of the Godhead dwelt in him—his perfect innocence—his deep humiliation—his obedience unto death, even the death of the cross—his conquest of death—his ascension to heaven and investiture with universal dominion—his present mediatorial kingdom; and his future descent from heaven to restore this part of God's creation, to destroy the workers of iniquity, and to gather the virtuous of all nations and times into that kingdom which was prepared for them from the foundation of the world—In short, he was, as they believe, that Son of God and great Messiah who had been promised from the creation, and was sent in the fullness of time to proclaim peace and favour to guilty men, to lead them to the knowledge of the only true God and to assure them of his placable character, to set before them the best example, to publish the covenant of grace, to confirm this

this covenant by his blood, to shew us the path of life in his own resurrection, and to take upon him that invisible government which, according to the Scriptures, he is now carrying on, and which is to terminate in the extirpation of sin and death, and the establishment of an everlasting kingdom of peace and virtue in another world.

The enumeration of these particulars is enough to shew you that there is no reason for that aversion with which many good men think of this scheme of Christianity. One of its chief peculiarities has been mentioned under the former head. Under this head I must observe to you, that, while its advocates admit all the facts just recited relating to the doctrine of our salvation by Christ, and therefore all that any good man need be very anxious about, they reject the common modes of interpreting this doctrine, and particularly the opinion that he saved us by making satisfaction to the justice of the Deity

Deity for our sins, and by suffering in himself the very punishment due to sinners in order to let them go free. He died for us, they say, not as a *substitute*, but as one man dies for another when he gives up his life in order to serve him. He died, not to reconcile *God* to *us*; but, on the contrary, to assure us of God's love, and to induce *us* to be reconciled to God. He was a sacrifice and a Redeemer, not by offering an equivalent or paying down a price, but by devoting himself in the cause of truth and virtue, and by sealing the covenant of grace and the promise of pardon which he published with his blood.

In these assertions there is a great deal that is true; for indeed nothing can be less reasonable than some of the explanations which have been given of our redemption by Christ. According to the most common of these explanations, sin being committed against an infinite being is an infinite evil, and deserves infinite punish-punifhment; and, confequently, none but an infinite being could make fatisfaction for it. Chrift, being a man making one perfon with the fecond perfon in the Trinity (and, therefore, having by this union infinite merit communicated to his fufferings) made this fatisfaction by fuffering and dying on the crofs. But he did not make it for *all*. On the contrary; though one drop of his blood was fufficient to purchafe univerfal falvation, it was fhed only for the elect; and the reft of mankind having had no fatisfaction made for their fins, were left in the ftate into which Adams's fall brought them; that is, in a ftate which fubjected them neceffarily, unlefs redeemed, to everlafting mifery.—God the Father was provoked, and required fatisfaction. God the Son ftepped in to appeafe him, and to make the required fatisfaction by his vicarious facrifice; excluding, however, from the benefit of it the greater part of mankind.

This is a juſt account of the ideas which many of our fellow chriſtians have entertained of the method of our ſalvation by Chriſt; and they lead us moſt abſurdly to conceive of one part of the Divine nature as making ſatisfaction to another part of it; and, therefore, this other part as itſelf left unſatisfied. It likewiſe follows from them, that our redemption having been bought, and the full price given for it, could not have been derived from the free grace of God. But what is worſt of all in this account of our redemption is, that, by repreſenting the Deity in the character of an angry and inexorable Judge, and Jeſus Chriſt in the oppoſite character of a mild and benevolent Pacifier and Friend, it tends to transfer our love from that Being, who is the Father of mercies and the firſt cauſe of all good, to that *Meſſenger* whom he ſent into the world to carry on the purpoſes of his goodneſs. Such ſentiments as theſe cannot be condemned too ſtrongly. It was neceſſary that on this

this occasion I should mention them to you in order to guard you against them. They are a wretched misconception of one of the most important of all doctrines; and they must have a very unhappy effect on the tempers of those who receive them, with respect to that *first* and *best*, as well as *greatest*, of all beings who is the proper object in all cases of our *first* and *best* regards.

But though, even on the subject of our redemption by Christ, I agree in this instance with that denomination of Christians whose opinions I am now describing, I can by no means think of it in every respect as they do. I believe Christ to be a Saviour in a much higher sense than they allow. I view his character in a much higher light. He died, they say, to bear witness to the truth, and to confirm the doctrine he taught by laying down his life for it; and he saves us by leading us to repentance and virtue, and by conveying to penitent sinners a remission of punishment and future happiness. I assent to this, but cannot think it the whole truth, as you will find when I have given you an account of the THIRD of those schemes into which I have divided the opinions of Christians concerning the Gospel, and which I shall now proceed to explain.

After what I have already said, a few words will be sufficient for this purpose.

This THIRD scheme agrees with the scheme last stated in all that relates to the nature of the Deity and the consequences of the fall; and also, in rejecting the doctrines of absolute predestination, particular redemption, irresistible grace, and justification by faith only. It differs from it principally on the two last of the *four* points I have mentioned; and I have called it the *middle* scheme, because, on these two points, it neither carries our sentiments so high as *Athanasianism* and *Calvinism*, nor sinks them so low as *Socinianism*

anism. It makes Christ more than a human being; his character more than that of a reformer; and our salvation by him more than a mere *conveyance* of benefits. It teaches that Christ descended to this earth from a state of pre-existent dignity; that he was in the beginning with God, and that by him God made this world; and that by a humiliation of himself which has no parallel, and by which he has exhibited an example of benevolence that passes knowledge, he took on him flesh and blood and passed through human life, enduring all its sorrows in order to save and bless a sinful race. By delivering himself up to death he acquired the power of delivering us from death. By offering himself a sacrifice on the cross he vindicated the honour of those laws which sinners had broken, and rendered the exercise of favour to them consistent with the holiness and wisdom of God's government; and by his resurrection from the dead he proved the efficacy and acceptableness of his sacrifice. In a word; according to this scheme, Christ not only *declared* but *obtained* the availableness of repentance to pardon; and became, by his interposition, not only the *Conveyer* but the *Author* and the *means* of our future immortality. This was a service so great that no meaner agent could be equal to it; and, in consequence of it, offers of full favour are made to all; no human being will be excluded from salvation except through his own fault; and every truly virtuous man from the beginning to the end of time (be his country or his religion what it will) is made sure of being raised from death and made happy for ever. It is necessary to add, that in all this the Supreme Deity, according to the same principles, is to be considered as the first cause, and Christ as his GIFT to fallen man; and as acting under that eternal and self-existent Being compared with whom no other being is either great or good, and *of whom and through whom and to whom are all things.*

This

This is the account of the Gospel which appears to me to be the nearest the truth; and, as it is a mean between two opposite schemes, it is more likely to deserve our preference. There are, however, some modifications of it which approach too nearly to the scheme first explained; and this, in my opinion, is true in particular of the account which has been given of the dignity of Christ and the doctrine of our redemption by the truly great and excellent Dr. Clarke. In the explications he gives of the doctrine of our redemption, he seems to have carried his ideas to substitution, satisfaction, and vicarious punishments: And he seems also to have held such a *pre-eminence* of Christ above all creatures, and such a peculiar manner of his derivation from God as is perfectly incomprehensible, and grounded on a misinterpretation of the language of Scripture. But I must not now dwell on such observations.

My busines in what remains of these discourses shall be to give you an account of the reasons which determine me to prefer this *third* scheme of Christianity to the *Socinian* scheme. In doing this I shall confine myself to the two points I have so often mentioned, and endeavour to state my reasons, *first* of all, for believing that Christ, with respect to his nature or person was *more* than a man; and, *secondly*, for believing that, with respect to his office as a Saviour, he was more than a teacher and example. At present I will only make a few observotions previous to the discussion of the first of these points.

First. I would point out to your notice a particular coincidence between *Socinianism* and the high *Trinitarian* doctrine. You will find, upon reflection, that there cannot be a more remarkable instance of a trite observation, " that extremes " are apt to meet." According to the *Athanasian* doctrine, that *Jesus* who was born of a virgin, who bled on the cross,

and

and who rose again, was simply a man feeling all our wants and subject to all our infirmities and sufferings. It is impossible that any one who has the use of his reason should believe that GOD was born, and suffered, and bled, and died. This was true only of the *man* Jesus. The contrary is too shocking to be even imagined; nor is it asserted by the advocates of the proper Deity of Jesus Christ. What they say is, that though Christ was *very man*, yet he was also *very God*; and when they say he was *very God* they do not mean that he lost his nature [e] as a *man*

by

[e] Dr. Horsley (in a sermon on the incarnation lately published) has made an observation on this subject which seems curious. According to him the hypostatical union could not have taken place if the principle of individual existence in the man Jesus had not been that union itself; and the necessity of this created the necessity of the miraculous conception, a man produced in the common way, or (as he speaks) by the physical powers of generation, being incapable of such an union.

by a conversion of it into the substance of the Deity (this also being an absurdity too gross to be admitted by any human mind) but that there was an *union* between it and the *Divine* nature which gave value and efficacy to the sufferings of the man. The *Socinians* say much the same; for they say, that God dwelt in Jesus and acted and spoke by him, and that there was such an extraordinary communication of Divine influence to him as raised him above other mortals and rendered him properly *God with us*, that is, God manifesting himself to us and displaying his power and perfections on earth in the person, discourses, and miracles of Christ. The advocates of the *Athanasian* doctrine cannot mean more than this by the *union* they talk of between God and Christ. They call it indeed an union of two natures into one person; an union which made the *Godhead* and the *manhood* one complex subject of action and passion. But this is *a language* to which they cannot

not poffibly fix any ideas: For, whatever they may pretend, they cannot really believe that *any* two natures, much lefs two natures fo effentially different as the human and Divine, can make *one* perfon; or that there could have been fuch an union between Jefus and the Supreme Deity as to make it ſtrictly true, that when *Jefus* was born, *God* was born; or that when *Jefus* was crucified, *God* was crucified. They are no more capable of believing this than the Papifts, when they maintain tranfubftantiation, are capable of believing that the body of Chrift may be eaten at one and the fame time in a million of places, or that Chrift at his laſt fupper really held his body in his hand and gave it to his apoftles. As far, therefore, as *Trinitarians* and *Socinians* have ideas they are agreed on this fubject; and the war they have been maintaining againſt one another has been entirely a war of words.—What an inftance is this

of

of human weakness? There are no two parties of Christians who talk languages about Christ more seemingly opposite; one maintaining zealously that he was the eternal God, and the other that he was a man; and yet when their ideas are examined we find that they coincide, the one making him in reality as much a mere man as the other, and the only difference being, that the one talk a plain language about the union of this man to the Deity; and that the other run it up to a mystery which admits of no explanation or meaning. But what is a still more melancholy proof of human weakness is the stress which one of these parties have laid on their mysterious doctrine; and the horrid barbarity with which, in former ages, they persecuted all who could not receive it. Even now, in this enlightened and happy country, there is (as you well know) a creed, in constant use and obstinately retained, which declares that without

out doubt all who reject this doctrine will perish everlastingly [g].

But

[g] There is an opinion concerning Christ which I have thought not necessary to be noticed in these discourses. It is the opinion in which a very amiable divine (the late Dr. WATTS) settled after spending many years in perplexing enquiries, and taking much pains to keep within the limits of the doctrines commonly reckoned orthodox. It agrees with *Arianism* in the *strange* doctrine, as Dr. Watts calls it *(*see his *Solemn Address to the Deity* in the 4th volume of his works) of a THREEFOLD Deity consisting of Father, Son, and Holy Ghost in one undivided essence; and in maintaining, that the Saviour who died for us was a super-angelic spirit, the first of God's productions and the limit between him and his creatures, and not a mere man, as *Athanasians* and *Socinians* say. But it differs from *Arianism* in asserting a doctrine which seems even *more* strange than that concerning the Deity which Dr. Watts rejected. I mean, the doctrine of a TWO-FOLD Christ consisting of *two* natures in *one* person; or of two beings (the self-existent Creator and a creature) made, as Dr. Watts speaks, in one complex being by an ineffable union and indwelling, which renders all the same titles, attributes, and honours, equally applicable to both. See Dr. *Watt's Treatise on the Glory of Christ as God-man.*

The

But secondly; another previous observation which I would make is, that tho', in opposition to the doctrine both of *Trinitarians* and *Socinians*, I look upon Christ as

The *Arian* part of this scheme (now generally distinguished by the name of the *indwelling* scheme) gave so much offence to Dr. Watt's more orthodox brethren, that the latter part of it could not save him from their censures, or make him an object of their charity. This should have taught *him* charity to all his less orthodox brethren. But it had not this effect. Concerning Socinians he intimates (in the Preface to his book entitled *Orthodoxy and Charity united*) that the Scriptures did not warrant him to extend his charity to them; and that they are exposed to a sentence from which he prays that the grace of God may recover and preserve them. In a Poem also *on Mr. Lock's Annotations* inserted among his *Lyric Poems*, he makes an apology for invoking the help of Charity to find Mr. Lock in heaven, by intimating that he could not have done this had he not concluded from his explanation of Rom. v. 21. that he was not a *Socinian*.—How strongly does this shew that allowances ought sometimes to be made even for uncharitableness? And what a proof is it of the unhappy influence of the prejudices to which we are as more than any human being, I do not presume to be able to determine the *degree* of his superiority, or to know any thing of the particular rank which he held in God's universe before his descent from heaven. This is a point which we have neither means for discovering, nor faculties for understanding. The Scriptures are in a great degree silent about it, informing us only that *he was before Abraham*; *that he had glory with God before the world was*; and that, thro' his intermediate agency, God made *this* world. I say *this* world, for you should never forget that when the Scriptures speak of the *world* they mean only *this* world with its connections and dependencies, the sacred writers having probably never carried their views farther,

or

are all liable, and which often contract and darken the best minds?—These prejudices would be exterminated, and all Christians would respect one another, were the doctrine I have endeavoured to inculcate in the first of these discourses universally received.

or formed any conception of those innumerable worlds and *systems* of worlds which have been discovered by the modern improvements in philosophy and astronomy. Those learned men, therefore, seem to me to have gone much too far, who (though they deny Christ's equality to his God and our God) yet speak of him as a Being who existed before *all worlds* and as at the head of *all worlds*. This seems almost as little warranted by reason and Scripture as the doctrine which makes him the ONE SUPREME; and it makes the doctrine of his having humbled himself to death even the death of the cross to save this world, almost equally incredible. When in the *Colossians* he is styled the *image of the invisible Deity, and the First-born of every creature*, the meaning is, that by the Divine power which he displayed he was a representation on earth of the ever blessed Deity; and that by rising from the dead he became, what he is elsewhere called, the First-fruits of them
that

that sleep, and the First-born from the dead of human beings,

Thirdly, There is one previous observation more which I would recommend to your particular consideration.

Amidst all the speculations and controversies about the person and offices of Christ, I wish you would never forget that the *only* object of religious worship is the one Supreme Deity. This, I think, a point of great consequence, There is no other being concerning whom we have sufficient reason to think, that he is continually present with us, and a witness to all our thoughts and desires. There is, therefore, no other being to whom our prayers ought to be directed. It was to this Being that our Lord himself directed his prayers. And his language to us is, *thou shalt worship the Lord thy God and him only shalt thou serve*, Mat. iv. 10. *You shall ask me nothing. Whatever ye shall ask the Father in my name, he will give it to you,* John xvi. 23. This is the Scripture rule of worship. We are to pray to God in the *name* of Christ; that is, as his disciples, and with a regard to him as the Mediator between God and man. To this purpose St. Paul exhorts us in Col. iii. 16. *Do every thing in the name of Christ, giving thanks to God and the Father by him.* The injunction to St. John, when he would have fallen down to worship the angel that shewed him the prophetical visions in the book of Revelation, we should consider as given to every Christian who is disposed to worship any being except the ONE SUPREME—*See thou do it not. Worship God.* All other worship is an idolatry which the Christian religion forbids. The proneness to it, however, among Christians, as well as Heathens, has been in all ages melancholy and shocking. The religion of Heathens consisted chiefly in the worship of human spirits supposed to have

have been elevated after their deaths into a participation with the Supreme Deity in the government of the world. The religion of *Papists* is in a great degree the same. Their prayers are directed much more to the Virgin *Mary*, and deified human spirits called *saints*, than to God. —Nor are *Protestants* guiltless. For, if the doctrine of the Trinity be false, what must the worship be that is grounded upon it? How much must the reformed churches themselves want reformation?— Even *Socinians* have not kept clear of this great error of Christendom[h]. You have heard that, in former times, they contended zealously for the obligation to invoke and worship Christ, though, in their

---

[h] It is remarkable that *Socinus*, whose zeal on this point was so great as to make him a persecutor, at the same time asserted that idolaters could not be saved. How happy is it for us, that even our own sentences here shall not condemn us hereafter, provided we are sincere?

their opinion, not a *creature* only, but a *mere man.*

Suffer me here to address you in the words with which the apostle John concludes his first Epistle—*Little children keep yourselves from idols.* Adhere to the worship of the one living and true God, and admit no other beings to a share with him in your adorations. That grand apostacy among Christians which is predicted in the New Testament, consists principally in their falling into idolatrous worship[1]. This

---

[1] The learned Mr. *Joseph Mede,* in the last century, has given an intimation of "Some sin which the "whole body of the reformation is guilty of, but "which is counted no sin." And Sir *Isaac Newton,* in his Commentary on the Revelations, speaks of "all nations having corrupted the Christian religion, "and of a recovery of the *long lost truth* which is to "be effected hereafter."—"I can by no means con- "ceive (says an excellent clergyman and valuable "writer) what it is these writers point at except it "be the supremacy of the God and Father of all, "which

This is that spiritual fornication for which the Jews were so often punished; and which, according to all the best commentators, has given the name of the *mother of harlots* to the church of *Rome*. Avoid it then carefully and anxiously. You cannot be wrong when you follow, in this and other instances, the example of Jesus Christ.

It is the conviction that the true object of religious worship is God the Father *only*, that in a great measure makes us *Protestant* Dissenters. Let us keep on this

---

" which they might possibly believe to be a truth
" that has been denied and lost by the general decla-
" ration of the churches, *that two other persons are*
" *his equals.* This is so far from being looked upon
" as a sin that it is a sign of orthodoxy, and is a
" doctrine that pervades the whole reformation."
See Reflections on the 15th chapter of Mr. *Gibbon*'s History, &c. p. 73, by the late Mr. Henry Taylor, Rector of Crawley, and Vicar of Portsmouth, Hants.

this ground. It is impossible we should find better. There are probably superior invisible beings without number. But we have nothing to do with them as objects of our devotions. Our invocations in prayer must be confined to that one self-existent being who governs all beings. There are other lords; but their authority is derived from him. There are other saviours, but they are his *gifts*; and of these the first and best is that Saviour who left heaven to deliver us from sin and death, and to lift us to a happy immortality. To this Saviour we owe an ardent gratitude; but the gratitude we owe to him is nothing compared with that which we owe to the God who gave him, and whom alone we know to be ever near us to hear and notice our prayers and praises.

Having made these previous observations, I shall next proceed to set before you some arguments which appear to me
to

to prove the two doctrines of the preexistent dignity of Christ, and his having performed a higher service for us than any being merely human could have performed. But this I must reserve for some future discourses.

SERMON IV.

OF THE PRE-EXISTENCE AND DIGNITY OF CHRIST.

1 JOHN iv. 14.

We have seen, and do testify, that the Father sent the Son to be the Saviour of the world.

IN discoursing to you on the different schemes of Christianity you may remember that (after shewing that we are all agreed with respect to the *essentials* of it, and the information which it was intended principally to communicate, and which is most interesting to us as sinful and dying creatures) I arranged the different sentiments which have been entertained

tained concerning it under three schemes, each of which I stated, giving the preference to that which I did not know how better to distinguish than by calling it the middle scheme between *Calvinism* and *Socinianism.*

My design, in what is to follow of these discourses, is to state the reasons which seem to me to shew that this scheme comes nearest the truth. At the close of my last discourse, I made some preparatory observations which I thought necessary; and, with this view, I

First pointed out to your notice a coincidence which there is, on the subject of Christ's dignity, between the opinions of *Trinitarians* and *Socinians.* Both make the Jesus who bled and died on the cross a *mere man*, but distinguished from *common men* by a miraculous conception and a particular communication of Divine powers. In opposition to this doctrine, I have proposed to state the reasons which lead me to believe, that he was *more* than a man, a man, and that he not only was endowed with extraordinary powers, but had existed before his appearance in this world in a state of dignity and glory.

Secondly; I desired you to observe that, while I believe this to be the truth, I do not mean to assert any thing with respect to the degree of our Lord's *pre-existent* dignity, this being a point about which the Scriptures are silent except by saying that God made this world by him.

Thirdly; I desired you to observe, that whatever may be the dignity of Christ or our obligations to him, the only object of our religious worship is that one Supreme Being who sent him into the world; and that all prayer directed to other beings is an idolatry which we ought anxiously to avoid.

I shall now proceed to state my reasons for receiving that account of the Gospel to which I have given the preference. It differs, I have said, from *Socinianism* in two

two particulars. First, in asserting Christ to have been more than any human being. And, secondly, in asserting that he took upon him human nature for a higher purpose than merely revealing to mankind the will of God, and instructing them in their duty and in the doctrines of religion. In discoursing on these subjects, I have thought the words I have just read to you better adapted to my views than the words on which I grounded my former discourses. *We have seen and do testify* (says St. John) *that the Father sent the Son to be the Saviour of the world.*—These words imply the following very important truths.

First; that Jesus Christ was the *Messenger* of God the Father Almighty; and that, therefore, we are to ascribe to him ultimately all that Christ did and all that we owe to him. The Father, my text says, SENT the Son.

Secondly, that this Messenger was one of peculiar excellence and dignity. By way of distinction, and in order to mark his

his peculiar eminence, he is called the SON. So likewise in the first verse of the Epistle to the Hebrews it is said that God, *who at sundry times and in divers manners spoke in times past to the fathers by the prophets, hath in these last times spoken to us by his* SON, *by whom he made the worlds.*

Thirdly; these words imply that Christ was sent into the world to perform for it a service of the last importance. He was sent to SAVE it. The Father sent the Son to be the SAVIOUR of the world.—These words, therefore, lead me to answer the following enquiries.

1st. Whether the peculiar dignity of Christ, as pointed out to us in the Sriptures, means any more than what *Athanasians* and *Socinians* say; that is, his being a man the same with ourselves, but in union with the Deity and endowed with extraordinary powers?

2dly. What the nature was of that *instrumentality* in the work of our redemption, which is expressed when it is said that

that God SENT him to be the Saviour of the world.

And 3dly. Whether he is a *Saviour* in any other way than by his inftructions and example.

Firft, let us enquire what reafons there are for believing that Chrift's peculiar dignity, as defcribed in the Scriptures, implies that he was more than any being merely human.

As one who wifhes to be a candid enquirer after truth, I muft here tell you, that I think the mere appellation *(Son of God)* applied to Chrift decides nothing on this fubject. The manner in which he is fo ftyled in my text and in other places of Scripture implies, as I have juft obferved, his *pre-eminence* as a Prophet and Meffenger from God; but the appellation, taken by itfelf and abftracted from the circumftances of its application, affords no proof of his being more than a man. It is indeed a phrafe which has been deplorably mif-misinterpreted; and on which a doctrine concerning God the most unintelligible has been grounded. By *Trinitarians* and *Calvinists*, it has been supposed to refer to an eternal derivation of one part of the Divine nature from another, or of the *second* person in the Trinity from the *first*; and their language is, that Christ was neither *made* nor *created*, but *begotten* from everlasting, and of one substance with the Father. And, even by many more rational divines, this phrase has been thought to refer to some peculiar manner in which Christ derived his existence from the Deity before all worlds, and by which he is distinguished from and raised above all the other productions of the Divine will and power. For this reason they think Christ is called the *Only* Begotten of the Father, there existing no other being derived from him in the same way; that is, by *generation*, and not by *creation*. There is scarcely any thing that strikes me more, with a conviction of the infirmity of the

human

human underftanding, than the zeal with which this moft groundlefs and abfurd notion has been received by fome of the ableft and beft men. That it is wholly groundlefs will appear from the following confiderations.

First; with refpect to the epithet *only-begotten* applied to Chrift as the Son of God, it is plain that it means no more than his being his *beloved* Son, as he is likewife often called in the Scriptures.— Thus is this epithet ufed in Prov. iv. 3. *For I was my father's fon tender and only* (that is, peculiarly) *beloved in the fight of my mother.* And it is remarkable, that the *Greek* tranflators of the Old Teftament frequently render the words which, in the original, fignify *only* fon, by *beloved* fon.

It deferves your notice here, that Chrift is ftyled God's *firft-begotten* as well as his *only-begotten* Son; and that he is fo ftyled plainly for no other reafon, than that he was the *firft* that rofe from the dead.

Thus

Thus Rev. i. 5. *Grace be to you from him which is and which was and which is to come; and from Jesus Christ the Faithful Witness, the First-Begotten from the dead, and the Prince of the kings of the earth* And Col. i. 18. *He is the Head of the church, the Beginning, the First-Born from the dead, that in all things he might have the pre-eminence.* Can any one imagine, that in these texts the sacred writers had any view to the mode of Christ's derivation from the Father before all worlds? It is equally unreasonable to imagine, they had any such view when they apply the title *Son of God generally* to him, without any epithet. In reality; it is only a particular kind of phraseology used in the Scriptures; and which is frequently applied to many besides our Saviour. Angels are styled the *Sons of God,* Job xxxviii. 7. *When the morning stars sang together, and all the sons of God shouted for joy.* See likewise Dan. iii. 25.—Adam is called the *son of God,* Luke iii. 38.—Magistrates are called the *sons of God*, Pſal. lxxxii. 6. and John x. 34.—Iſrael is called God's *firſt-born*, Exod. iv. 22. *And thou ſhalt ſay unto Pharoah; thus ſaith the Lord; Iſrael is my ſon, even my firſt-born.*—But this title is, in a more particular manner, applyed to good men and virtuous Chriſtians in the New Teſtament. *As many as are led by the ſpirit of God,* St. Paul tells us, *are the ſons of God; and if ſons, then heirs; heirs of God, and joint heirs with Chriſt,* Rom. viii. 14, and 17. So likewiſe, Rev. xxi. 7. *He that overcometh ſhall inherit all things, and I will be his God, and he ſhall be my ſon.* And in John i. 12. it is ſaid that to *as many as receive Chriſt, he gave the power to become the ſons of God.*

In ſhort; according to the Scripture language, we are all the ſons of God; but Chriſt is ſo more particularly and eminently. God is the Father of us all, as well as of Chriſt; but he is the firſt-born among many brethren, having God for *his* God no leſs than he is *our* God. *I aſ-*
cend

cend (said our Saviour to Martha) *to my God and to your God, to my Father and to your Father.*

The title *Son of God* then being applicable to Christ, with all the epithets added to it, were he only a man, nothing can be inferred from it with respect to his pre-existent dignity. And this will appear yet more plainly from considering, that he is styled in the Scriptures the *Son of Man* as well as the *Son of God*; and that both these titles took their rise from two remarkable prophecies in the Old Testament concerning the Messiah. The first took its rise from *Daniel* the 7th chapter and 13th verse. *I saw in the night visions, and behold one like the* SON OF MAN *came with the clouds of heaven to the Ancient of days; and there was given him dominion and glory and a kingdom that all people and nations and languages should serve him.* The latter took its rise from the prophecy in the three first verses of the 42d chapter of Isaiah. *Behold my* SERVANT (or, as it is quoted in Mat. xii. 18.) *Behold my* Son *whom I have chosen, my Beloved in whom my soul delighteth. I will put my spirit upon him, and he shall shew forth judgment to the Gentiles.* But it will be proper to be more explicit here, and to observe that Christ is called the Son of God on three accounts in the New Testament.

First. On account of his miraculous conception. This is evident from Luke i. 35. *The angel said to her, the Holy Ghost shall come upon thee. The power of the Highest shall overshadow thee. Therefore, that holy thing which shall be born of thee shall be called the* Son of God.

Secondly. On account of his resurrection. This appears from Rom. i. 4. *Declared to be the Son of God with power by his resurrection from the dead.* And more plainly from Acts xiii. 33. *The promise which was made to our fathers, God hath fulfilled to us their children, in that he hath raised up Jesus from the dead, as it is written in the second*

second Pfalm. *Thou art my Son; this day have I begotten thee.*

Thirdly. On account of his office as the Meſſiah. In conſequence of Iſaiah's prophecy juſt quoted, the phraſe *Son of God* came to be the moſt common title by which the Meſſiah was characterized among the Jews. So true is this, that it appears plainly in the Goſpel hiſtory that theſe two titles, the *Son of God* and the *Meſſiah*, were ſynonimous among the Jews at the time of our Lord's public miniſtry. When St. John at the end of his Goſpel declares, that what he had written was in order *that they might believe that Jeſus was the Chriſt, the Son of God*; it is plain that he uſes the phraſe *Son of God* as only another phraſe for the *Chriſt*, that is, the *Meſſiah*. The ſame is true of Nathanael's declaration on ſeeing our Saviour. *Rabbi, thou art the Son of God. Thou art the King of Iſrael.* And alſo, of the confeſſion made by the demoniacs mentioned Luke iv. 41. *Demons alſo came out of many crying out* and saying, *Thou art the Messiah, the Son of God.* When the Jews asked our Lord, Luke xxii. 70. *Art thou the Son of God?* their meaning undoubtedly was, *Art thou the Messiah?* And thus that very question is expressed in Mark xiv. 61. *Art thou the Messiah, the Son of the blessed* [a]*?*

It would be wasting your time to say more on this subject. Such is the true account of a phraseology in Scripture which has nothing in it that is not easy and intelligible; but which has, among *Christians,* produced some of the grossest conceptions of the Deity; and among *Infidels* exposed Christianity to ridicule and scorn.

Having thus shewn you that no conclusion, with respect to the doctrine of Christ's pre-

---

[a] The account here given of Christ's being called the Son of God, is nearly the same with that given by Dr. Watts in his Treatise entitled, *Useful and Important Questions concerning Jesus the Son of God freely proposed, with a humble attempt to answer them.*

pre-exiftence, can be drawn merely from his being called the *Son of God*, I fhall now ftate to you thofe reafons which influence my judgment in this inftance, and which feem to me to prove this doctrine.

Firft, I will obferve that the denial of it feems, in a great meafure, derived from narrow ideas of the extent of the creation, and of the connections and dependencies that take place in it. We are too apt to look upon ourfelves as placed by ourfelves on this globe, as unconnected with any fuperior world of fpirits, and the fun and ftars as made only for us. This is all miferable narrownefs and fhortfightednefs. That earth, which appears to us fo great, is (comparatively fpeaking) nothing to the folar fyftem: The folar fyftem, nothing to the fyftem of the fixed ftars: And the fyftem of the fixed ftars nothing to that fyftem of fyftems of which it is a part.—I refer now to fome difcoveries in the heavens which have been lately

lately made. The planets are so many inhabited worlds; and all the stars which twinkle in the sky so many suns enlightening other worlds. This no one now doubts. But late observations have carried our views much farther, by discovering that this whole vast collection of worlds and systems bears a relation to other collections of worlds and systems; that our system moves towards other systems; that all the visible frame of sun, planets, stars, and milky-way forms one *cluster* of systems; and that, in the immense expanse of the heavens, there are myriads of these clusters which to common glasses appear like small white clouds, but to better glasses appear to be assemblages of stars mixing their light. This sets before us a prospect which turns us giddy; but, however astonishing, we have reason to believe that all that it presents to us is *nothing* to the real extent and grandeur of the universe; for all these myriads of words, of *systems* of worlds, and of *assemblages*

semblages of systems being formed so much on one plan as all to require *light*, it is more than probable that somewhere in the immensity of space, other plans of nature take place; and that, far beyond all that it is possible for us to descry, numberless scenes of existence are exhibited different in this respect, and of which we can no more form a notion than a child in the womb can form a notion of the solar system, or a man born blind of light and colours. But I am in danger of going farther than is suitable to my present purpose in speaking on this subject. What I have just said relates chiefly to *corporeal* nature; and my design has been to lead you to this reflection—
" That since *corporeal* nature is thus ex-
" tensive and grand; *incorporeal* nature,
" (that is, the *intellectual* universe) must
" be much more so." The former is in *itself* of no value. The *material* universe is the lowest part of created existence, and designed only to be the seat and receptacle of living and spiritual beings. These

spiritual

spiritual beings rise above one another in endless gradation from the oyster to the ONE SUPREME. They have, undoubtedly, connections and dependencies like those which are established in the material universe. Man, in particular, is only one link in this chain. It would be the greatest folly to imagine that he stands alone; or that he has no connections with superior orders of creatures. His present state may be derived from these connections; and the administration of the Divine government with respect to him may have a reference to them, and be in some manner dependent upon them. The Scriptures, I think, teach us plainly that this is the truth, by the account they give us of the fall, of angels good and bad, and of the *Messiah*. Nor can any doctrine appear more credible to a person who attends properly to the order and laws of the creation.

We see the whole of existence *below* us (that is, between man and nothing) filled with

with a variety, almoſt infinite, of different claſſes of beings all related and connected. Who can doubt whether all *above* us is alike full?—Let us here think of the poſſible dignity of ſuperior intelligent beings.

It is ſelf-evident, that the Almighty Being who exiſted from eternity might have exerted his power from eternity; and to aſſert the contrary is to aſſert that he muſt have paſſed an eternity *without* power.—But not to inſiſt on this, it will come to the ſame to ſay, that from a time in paſt duration, at a greater diſtance than any aſſignable, he has been exerting his Almighty power and perfect goodneſs. There are, therefore, reaſonable beings who have exiſted from indefinite ages. During all theſe ages they have been growing and riſing. What then muſt they *now* be? To what dignity muſt they have arrived? Of what conſequence muſt their agency be in the creation?—We are OURSELVES (ſhould we not loſe our exiſtence

istence by vice) to exist and to rise through eternal ages. What dignity then shall we *ourselves* some time or other reach? What importance must *our* agency some time or other acquire?

But to come to some evidences more to my present purpose.

I would observe, Secondly, that the history of our Saviour as given in the New Testament, and the events of his life and ministry, answer best to the opinion of the superiority of his nature.—Of this kind are his introduction into the world by a miraculous conception; the annunciations from heaven at his baptism and transfiguration proclaiming him the Son of God, and ordering all to hear him; his giving himself out as come from God to offer his life for the life of the world, and to shed his blood for the remission of sins; his *perfect* innocence and sinless example; the wisdom which discovered itself in his doctrine, and by which he spoke as never
man

man spoke; that knowledge of the hearts of men by which he could speak to their thoughts as we do to one another's words; his intimations that he was greater than Abraham, Moses, David, or even angels [b]; those miraculous powers by which, with a command over nature like that which first produced it, he ordered tempests to cease, and gave eyes to the blind, limbs to the maimed, reason to the frantic, health to the sick, and life to the dead; his surrender of himself to the enemies who took away his life, after demonstrating that it was his own consent [c] gave them

[b] *But of that day knoweth no man; no not the angels which are in heaven, neither the* SON, *but the Father only*, Mark xiii. 32.

[c] See John xviii. 14, &c. There was unspeakable dignity in our Lord's conduct as described in this passage. The band of officers and soldiers who came to apprehend him, struck by invisible power, were thrown backward and fell to the ground upon approaching him. After this it is probable they were afraid of again approaching him. He was, therefore,

them their power over him; the signs which accompanied his sufferings and death; his resurrection from the dead and triumphant ascension to heaven.—Never was a character so august exhibited on the stage of this world [d].—The Evangelists have

fore, obliged to offer himself to them, and to desire they would take him. He saw now before him a dreadful scene of humiliation and torture. In a few hours he was to be nailed to a cross, and to be held up before a whole kingdom as an object of insult. In these circumstances, it was proper there should be demonstrations given of his superiority and greatness. When he suffered nature seemed to suffer with him. The earth shook, and the light of day withdrew itself. And after hanging on the cross a sufficient time, and crying with a loud voice *it is finished*, he bowed his head and dismissed his spirit (παρεδωκε το πνευμα.) This was dying as no one ever died. It verified his declaration that *no one took his life from him; but that he gave it up of himself.*

[d] This is a subject which has been well treated by some of our best writers, and particularly by Doctor Newcombe, the learned and excellent Bishop of Waterford, in his *Observations on our Lord's conduct as a Divine Instructor.*

have drawn it by the recital of facts only, without any appearance of art or effort. And when I contemplate it in all its circumstances, I am disposed indeed to cry out, in language similar to that of the Roman centurion who attended his crucifixion, " Surely this was a superior being."

You must be sensible that I mention this as a presumptive argument only. It is, indeed, a consideration of some weight with me, that had a superior being come down from heaven for some purpose worthy of his interposition, the events recorded of Christ are just such as we might have reasonably expected would have bore witness to his greatness, and marked his entrance into the world, his passage through it, and his departure from it. Some, however, of the facts I have mentioned afford more than a presumptive argument. Such, in particular, is that *immaculateness* of character which the Scriptures ascribe to him. This, I think,
the

the Socinians in general allow. But it is conceivable that it could have belonged to a mere man [e]?—Another fact of the same kind is his raising *himself* from the dead. This he seems to have intimated when he said

[e] Chrift, if *impeccable* and *infallible* (as *Socinians* as well as other Chriftians have hitherto believed) muft have been not fimply a man like ourfelves, but (fuppofing him not to have pre-exifted) an angelic being created on purpofe at the time of his conception, and endowed immediately with the powers and knowledge of a fuperior being, without any of thofe previous acquifitions and gradual advances, which the natures of things as well as the ufual courfe of the Divine government, feem to require.—What can be lefs probable than a creation fo extraordinary?—The creation of an *Unique* amongft men; and for a purpofe too, which a man, fallible and peaceable like ourfelves, might have anfwered as well; and, in fome refpects, even better!—Compare with this, the defcent from heaven to give life to the world of a being who had before rifen to high powers.—How different, as to credibility as well as dignity, are the miffion and character of Chrift according to thefe different accounts of them?

A modern

said to the Jews,—" *Destroy this temple,* " *and in three days I will raise it up again;*" but more expresly in John x. 11, 18. *Therefore doth my Father love me because I lay*

A modern Socinian of the first character and ability appears to have felt this difficulty, and, therefore, has suggested that Christ was peccable and fallible like ourselves; and so much so, as to have been misled by vulgar prejudices, and capable of misapplying the Scriptures of the Old Testament—to have been conquered by the prospect of his crucifixion to a degree that shewed less fortitude than has been shewn by some common men in similar situations, tho' he foresaw his own immediate resurrection and the glory that was to follow it—to have been ignorant, before his baptism, of his own character as the Messiah; and, like the prophets that proceded him, even inferior in knowledge (except as far as he was taught by inspiration) to an enlightened man in modern times.—See *Observations on the Inspiration of Christ* in the Theological Repository, vol. iv. p. 435, &c. The Scripture assertion, that Christ knew no sin, means much the same, according to this author, with St. John's assertion (1 John iii. 9.) that a true Christian *cannot commit sin*, that is, cannot commit any acts of gross sin.

How-

lay down my life that I may take it again. No one taketh it from me; but I lay it down of myself. I have power to lay it down, and I have power to take it again. This commandment have I received of my Father.—In all other places GOD is said to have raifed Chrift

However contrary this account of Chrift may be to the general faith of Chriftians, I muft think, that it fhews the good fenfe of the writer, and is the only ground on which the *Socinian* doctrine is tenable.— The confequence, however, of thus lowering Chrift *before* his death is the neceffity of lowering him likewife *fince* his death. And, accordingly, this able writer, whofe candour appears to be fuch as will not fuffer him to evade any fair inference from his opinions, has farther intimated (*Ib.* p. 458) that Chrift's *judging the world* may mean lefs than is commonly believed, and perhaps the fame that is meant in 1 Cor. vi. 2. when it is faid, that the *faints are to judge the world.*—I hope, that fome time or other he will have the goodnefs to oblige the public by explaining himfelf on this fubject; and when he does, I hope he will farther fhew, how much lefs than is commonly believed, we are to underftand by Chrift's RAISING THE WORLD FROM THE DEAD.

Chrift from the dead; and thefe words inform us how this is to be underftood. God raifed Chrift from the dead by giving him a power to raife *himfelf* from the dead, and not only himfelf but all the world; or (as it is expreffed in chap. xx. 26.) by *giving to the Son of man to have life in himfelf, that as the Father raifeth up the dead and quickeneth them, fo might the Son quicken whom he will; the Father now judging no man, but having committed all judgment to the Son.* It is in this fenfe, the Scripture tells us fometimes, that *God* is to raife the dead hereafter, while yet its common language is, that *Chrift* is to raife the dead—But

Thirdly, It feems to me that there are in the New Teftament exprefs and direct declarations of the pre-exiftent dignity of Chrift. Of this fort I reckon the following paffages—John i. 1. compared with the 14th verfe. *In the beginning was the word, and the word was with God,* &c. *And the word was made flefh and dwelt among*

us.—John iii. 13. *No one hath ascended up to heaven, but he that came down from heaven; even the Son of Man who is in heaven.* —John vi. 62. *What and if ye shall see the Son of Man ascend up where he was before*[f].
—John

[f] In this chapter we find that our Lord took occasion, from the miracle of the loaves and fishes, to speak of himself as the true bread which was *come down from heaven* to give life to the world. The Jews understood this to be an intimation that he had existed in heaven before he came into this world, and therefore murmured at him and said (ver. 42.) Is not this Jesus the son of Joseph whose father and mother we know? How is it then that he says, I came down from heaven?—There is, in this case, a presumption that the sense in which the Jews understood our Lord was the most obvious and natural sense. If, however, it was not, and the Jews had perversely misinterpreted his words, it was reasonable to expect that he would have said something to correct their mistake: But, instead of this, we find that in his reply he repeated the same declaration in stronger language, and intimated that they had understood him rightly— Verse 61. *Does this offend you? What and if ye shall see the Son of Man ascend up where he was before?*

A like

—John viii. 58. *Before Abraham was, I am.*—And John xvii. 5. *And now O Father, glorify thou me with the glory which I had with thee before the world was.*

A like observation may be made on the words in John viii. 18. *Before Abraham was, I am.* It is in this instance also a circumstance of some consequence, that these words were occasioned by an offence which Jesus had given the Jews by an expression which they thought implied, that he had existed in the days of Abraham. Ver. 57. *Then said the Jews to him, Thou art not fifty years old, and hast thou seen Abraham? Jesus answered, Verily, verily, I say unto you, before Abraham was, I am.*

The whole context in which the words next quoted stands, is as follows.—*These words spake Jesus, and lifted up his eyes to heaven and said. Father, the hour is come. Glorify the Son that thy Son may also glorify thee; as thou hast given him power over all flesh that he should give eternal life to as many as thou hast given him. And this is life eternal that they may know thee the only true God, and Jesus Christ whom thou hast sent. I have glorified thee on earth. I have finished the work which thou gavest me to do. And now, O Father, glorify thou me with thine own self, with the glory which I had with thee before the world was.*—It seems to me that in this pas-

The limits to which I muſt confine myſelf will not allow me to enter into a critical examination of theſe texts. The interpretations which the Socinians give of them are ſuch as cannot eaſily occur to any plain man. Some of them have ſaid that Chriſt was taken up to heaven at the commencement of his public miniſtry; and that it is to this he refers when he ſpeaks of his coming down from heaven, and having been in heaven. But this is a groundleſs aſſertion which has been given up by modern Socinians, who maintain that theſe phraſes ſignify only Chriſt's having been ſent

ſage Chriſt has, with particular propriety and wiſdom, added to the declaration that power over all fleſh (or as he ſpeaks in Matth, xxviii. 18. all power in heaven and earth) was given him, an intimation of his having exiſted before this world was made. Such a declaration muſt have otherwiſe appeared extravagant. For what could be more extravagant than to ſuppoſe that ſo high a power could belong to ſuch a helpleſs and impotent creature of yeſterday as a mere man?—But more to this purpoſe will be ſaid preſently.

sent of God into the world, and having had communications from him. By his being *made* flesh they think no more is meant than that he *was* flesh and appeared in the world as a man. By saying that he existed before Abraham, they think he only meant that his existence was *intended* before Abraham; and by the *glory which he had with the Father before the world was*, they understand the glory which he had, in the Divine *foresight* and *appointment*, before the world was.—I must own to you, that I am inclined to wonder that wise and good men can satisfy themselves with such explanations.—But I correct myself. I know that Christians, amidst their differences of opinion, are too apt to wonder at one another; and to forget the allowances which ought to be made for the darkness in which we are all involved. Sensible of this truth, and hoping to be excused if I should ever express my convictions in too strong language, I proceed to recite to you some other texts which seem to be no lefs clear than thofe I have juft quoted.—Heb. ii. 9. *Jefus, who was made a little lower than the angels, that he might tafte death for every man.* And verfe 16. *He took not on him the nature of* (he helped not) *angels; but he took on him* (he helped) *the feed of Abraham.* Confider here how abfurd it would be to mention, as an inftance of condefcenfion and merit in a mere man, that he fubmitted to be made lower than the angels, and that he affifted not *them* but the feed of *Abraham?*—Of the fame kind, though not fo expreffive, are the words in Gal. iv. 4. *God fent forth his fon made of a woman;* and in 1 John iv. 2. *Jefus Chrift is come in the flefh.* This language is perfectly proper on the fuppofition of Chrift's pre-exiftence; but very improper on the contrary fuppofition: For how could a mere man be otherwife *made* than of a woman; or *come* otherwife than in the flefh?

Again; 2 Cor. viii. 9. *Ye know the grace of our Lord Jefus Chrift, that though he was rich*

rich yet for our sakes he became poor, that we through his poverty might be made rich.— When did our Lord possess riches? When did he exchange riches for poverty in order to make us rich? In this world he was always poor and persecuted.—But, in my opinion, the most decisive text of all is that in Phil. ii. and the 5th and following verses: *Let the same mind be in you that was in Christ; who, being in the form of God, thought it no robbery to be equal with God, but made himself of no reputation.* There is an incoherence in these words which shews they are not a right translation; and it is generally agreed among the best commentators that the true rendering is as follows. *Who being in the form of God did not covet to be honoured as God*[g]*, but divested himself, and took on him the form of a servant, and was made in the likeness of men; and being found in fashion as a man, humbled him-*

---

[g] See Dr. Clark's Scripture Doctrine of the Trinity, chap. xi. sect. 5. N° 934.

himself to death, even the death of the cross. I have often considered carefully the interpretation which the Socinians give of these words; and the more I have considered it the more confirmed I have been in thinking it forced and unnatural. The sense they give is this— *Who being in the form of God* (by the power which he possessed of working miracles) did not chuse to retain that power and so to appear like God, but divested himself of it, and took on him the form of a servant *and was made in the likeness of men.* Here they add the epithet ORDINARY, and read this passage as if it had been — *And was made in the likeness of an* ORDINARY *man; and, being found in fashion as an* ORDINARY *man, humbled himself to death.*—It is natural to ask here, When did Christ divest himself of the power of working miracles? The Gospel history tells us that he retained it to the last; and that he was never more distinguished than when at his crucifixion the earth shook, the rocks were split, and the

the fun was darkened?—Indeed the turn and ſtructure of this paſſage are ſuch, that I find it impoſſible not to believe, that the humiliation of Chriſt which St. Paul had in view was (not his exchanging one condition on earth for another) but his exchanging the glory he had with God before the world was for the condition of a man, and leaving that glory to encounter the difficulties of human life, and to ſuffer and die on the croſs. This was, in truth, an event worthy to be held forth to the admiration of Chriſtians. But if the apoſtle means only that Chriſt (though exalted above others by working miracles) yet conſented to ſuffer and to die like other men; if, I ſay, St. Paul means only this, the whole paſſage is rendered cold and trifling, no more being ſaid of Chriſt than might have been ſaid of St. Paul himſelf, or any of the other apoſtles [h].

There

---

[h] He who wiſhes to be aſſiſted, in judging how far the texts which I have here quoted can be reconciled

to

There remain to be quoted the texts which mention the creation of the world by Jesus Christ.—In Heb. i. 2. we read that God who, in former times spoke to the

to the *Socinian* doctrine, should consult Mr. LINDSEY's interpretations of them in the sequel to his Apology on resigning the vicarage of *Catterick*, Yorkshire; and also, the second of the two Essays in the fourth number of the *Commentaries and Essays published by the Society for promoting the Knowledge of the Scriptures.*

The passages of Scripture which call Christ a *man*, and in which he is said to have been *born*, have been insisted upon as making strongly for the *Socinian* doctrine. But this is an argument which makes no impression upon me. According to all opinions, Christ was *truly* a man, and is properly so called. Had the Scriptures called him a man, and added that he was *no more* than a man, this question would have been decided; but they have, I think, plainly enough asserted the contrary.—That humiliation of Christ, and suspension of his powers, which is implied in his being made a man and growing up, from infancy to mature age, subject to all our wants and sorrows, is indeed, as to the *manner* of it, entirely incomprehensible to us. But is this to be wondered at the fathers by the prophets, *hath in these last times spoken to us by his Son whom he hath appointed heir of all things; and by whom also he made the worlds.* Again; in the Gospel of John i. 3. it is said, that *the word was in the beginning with God; and that all things were made by him; and that without him nothing was made that was made.* —And, in the tenth verse, *That he was in the world, and that the world was made by him, but the world knew him not.*—And in Col. i. 16. *By him were all things created that are in heaven and that are in earth, visible and invisible* [i].

This at considering our ignorance of the nature of matter and spirit, and of the laws which govern the superior invisible world? Are we not continually witnesses to facts in some degree similar to this?—In short; those who will believe nothing the *manner and causes* of which they cannot comprehend, must be in the way to believe nothing at all.

[i] It is a circumstance a little discouraging in reciting this evidence from Scripture, that some modern *Socinians* would not be convinced by it were it ever

This is a fact that raises our ideas of the pre-existent dignity of Christ higher than any thing else that is said of him in the New Testament. But it is, in general, ever so clear and decisive. I find a proof of this in a late publication by a highly valued friend, and one of the most distinguished writers of the present times. Dr. Priestley, in the Introduction to his *History of the early Opinions concerning Christ,* has given such an explanation of the texts which seem to declare the creation of the world by Christ as he thinks may reconcile them to the Socinian doctrine. But, at the same time, he intimates, that had this been the opinion of the apostles we should not be bound to receive it. " As it is not pretended, he says, page 63,
" vol. i. that there are any miracles adapted to prove
" that Christ made and supports the world, I do not
" see that we are under any obligation to believe it
" merely because it was an opinion held by an apostle"
—And p. 70. " It is not, certainly, from a few casual
" expressions, which so easily admit of other inter-
" pretations, and especially in *epistolary* writings,
" that we can be authorized to infer that such was
" the serious opinion of the apostles. But if it had
" been their real opinion, it would not follow that it
" was true, unless the teaching of it should appear

neral, misinterpreted. In order to understand it properly, we should remember

First, that the term *world* in Scripture means only *this* world; and that *all things* mean only *all things* belonging to this world. The apostles probably never thought of that plurality of worlds which has been lately discovered. Indeed, had their minds been thus far enlightened, they would only have been embarrassed, and no good end could have been answered.—This earth, with its inhabitants and con-

" to be included in their general commission, with
" which, as I have shewn, it has no sort of connec-
" tion."

I have here, and every where else in these discourses, called the believers in the simple humanity of Christ *Socinians*, for want of knowing how better to distinguish them. They chuse to be called *Unitarians*. But they have no *exclusive right* to this title; ond *former Socinians* had *no* right to it at all; for they concurred with *Trinitarians* in worshipping a *deified* man.—It is an essential point of religion with me to worship God only.

connections, includes all of nature that we have any concern with; and it would be folly to imagine that the Scripture history and doctrines have any view to other worlds.—This obfervation is applicable to the account of the creation in the firft chapter of Genefis; that account, moft probably, being an account only of the creation of this earth with its immediate dependencies.

Secondly, You fhould remember that the formation of this world by Chrift does not imply *creation from nothing*, that probably being peculiar to Almighty power; but only an arrangement of things into their prefent order, and the eftablifhment of that courfe of nature to which we are witneffes.

Again. You fhould remember that Chrift is reprefented, not as the *original* creator, but as God's minifter in creation. God made the world (this is the language of Scripture but he made it *by* or *through* Chrift. The agency of Chrift, in this

in-

inftance is reprefented as entirely inftrumental, like that agency of his in working miracles which he defcribes when he fays, *I can of mine own felf do nothing. The Father who dwelleth in me, he doth the works.*—It is the conftant method of God's government, as far as it falls under our notice, to employ fubordinate agency in bringing about events; and, had I wanted in this cafe the authority of Scripture, I fhould have thought it highly probable, that it was by fuch agency the changes among worlds are often produced; and, in particular, that this globe was reduced from a chaotic ftate to its prefent habitable form, that mankind and other animals were planted upon it, and the laws fettled by which it is governed [k].

I can-

---

[k] Even men, in this earlieft ftage of their exiftence, poffefs a power (conftantly on the increafe) of changing the face of nature, and of introducing on this globe new fcenes of being and enjoyment, which is not totally unlike a power of raifing new creations.

I cannot help taking this opportunity to add, that the doctrine of God's forming this world by the agency of the Messiah gives a credibility to the doctrine of his interposition to save it, and his future agency in *new*-creating it; because it leads us to conceive of him as standing in a particular relation to it, and having an interest in it.

It is time to proceed to the next argument which I would offer.—It appears to me, that the doctrine of Christ's simple humanity, when viewed in connection with the Scripture account of his exaltation, implies an inconsistency and improbability which falls little short of an impossibility; and, consequently, that this doctrine not only renders the Scripture *unintelligible*, but Christianity itself *incredible.*—The Scriptures tell us that Christ, after his resurrection, became Lord of the dead and living; that he had all power given him in in heaven and earth; that angels were made subject to him; and that he is hereafter to raise all the dead, to judge the world, and to finish the scheme of the Divine moral government with respect to this earth, by conferring eternal happiness on all the virtuous, and punishing the wicked with *everlasting destruction.*— Consider whether such an elevation of a mere man is *credible,* or even *possible?* Can it be believed that a mere man could be advanced at once so high as to be above angels, and to be qualified to rule and judge this world? Does not this contradict all that we see, or can conceive of the order of God's works? Do not all beings rise gradually, one acquisition laying the foundation of another and preparing for higher acquisitions? What would you think were you told, that a child just born, instead of growing like all other human creatures, had started at once to complete manhood, and the government of an empire? This

This is nothing to the fact I am considering.—The power, in particular, which the Scriptures teach us that Christ possesses of raising to life all who *have* died and all who *will* die, is equivalent to the power of creating a world. How inconsistent is it to allow to him one of these powers, and at the same time to question whether he could have possessed the other?—to allow that he is to restore and *new-create* this world; and yet to deny that he might have been God's agent in originally forming it[1]?

Ac-

---

[1] Our brethren among modern *Socinians* seem to feel this difficulty; and therefore give a new interpretation of the Scripture account of Christ's present power and dignity.—Mr. LINDSEY says, in his Sequel, page 466, &c. that the exaltation of Christ to God's right-hand, *far above all might and dominion, and every name that is named, not only in this world but in that which is to come; angels, authorities, and powers being made subject to him*; is spoken of in accommodation to the ideas of the Jews and Gentiles of those days who believed there were such spiritual beings as angels and demons,

and Dignity of Chrift.

According to fome of the old Socinian writers, Chrift, after his refurrection, reigned over all nature, and became the object demons, and means only the difplay of a Divine power in the fupport of the Gofpel and its eftablifhment among men. The throne to which Chrift was advanced was, according to him (*Ib.* p. 243.) not any ftation of dignity in heaven, but the fubjection of the world to his Gofpel; and his glory with the father, mentioned John xvii. 5. was the glorious fuccefs of the Gofpel. *His power over all flefh* (John xvii. 2.) *to give eternal life to as many as the Father had given him,* was only his power " to afford men full af-
" furance of the benevolent purpofe of God to beftow
" eternal life upon them, and to furnifh them with
" the means of virtue that lead to it." P. 249.
" Agreeably to the prejudices and imaginations of
" Jews and Gentiles, the fubjection of all mankind
" to the rules of piety and virtue delivered by Chrift
" is fhadowed out under the imagery of a mighty
" king to whom all power was given in heaven and
" earth, placed above angels, principalities, &c."
P. 473. However fingular thefe interpretations may appear, no one ought haftily to condemn them, without confidering what fo excellent a man fays to juftify them in the paffages to which I have referred. It
is

object of religious worship [m]. It is surprising that men so enlightened on religious subjects as to be the wonder of the times in which they lived, did not feel the extravagance there is in ascribing to a mere man an advancement so sudden and astonish-

is probable that he interprets in a like sense Christ's declaration that he is the RESURRECTION AND THE LIFE, and understands by it only his being the REVEALER of a future life. But I shall indeed wonder if his good sense and candour will allow him to give the same sense to such texts as the following.—John vi. 40. *And I will raise him up at the last day.*—John v. 29. *The hour is coming in which all that are in their graves shall hear the voice of the Son of Man and shall come forth; they that have done good to the resurrection of life, and they that have done evil to the resurrection of damnation.*—Phil. v. 20, 21. *Our conversation is in heaven, from whence we look for the Saviour, the Lord Jesus Christ; who shall change our vile body that it may be fashioned like unto his glorious body, according to the working whereby he is able even to subdue all things to himself.*

[m] Christus ad dextram dei in cælis collocatus etiam ab angelis adorandus est. *Catachesis Ecclesiarum Polonicarum*, sect. 4. Omnem in cælo et in terra potestatem accepit; et omnia, Deo solo excepto, ejus pedibus sunt subjecta. *Ibid.*

aſtoniſhing. I do not think that there is, in *Athanaſianiſm* itſelf, any thing more extravagant. It is a circumſtance much in favour of Chriſtianity that, inſtead of aſſerting any ſuch doctrine, it teaches us that the ſame Chriſt who after his reſurrection had all power given him in heaven and earth, poſſeſſed *glory with God before the world was*; and that, when he aſcended to heaven, he only regained a former ſtation, and entered upon a dignity to which he had long riſen, with ſuch *additions* to it and ſuch *encreaſed* powers, as were the proper effect and reward of his having paſſed through human life to ſave the world.

The inconſiſtency of the Socinian doctrine will, in this inſtance, appear more palpable, if we will conſider what the *merit* was for which a mere man was thus exalted; and what the *end* was for which a ſtep ſo extraordinary was taken, and an effort ſo violent made. His merit was, ſacrificing his life in bearing witneſs to the truth; a merit by no means peculiar to him, many other men having done the same. The end was, the conveyance of blessings which would have been granted (because proper to be granted) whether conveyed by him or not, But on this subject, a good deal more will be said hereafter.

Fifthly. The doctrine I am considering lessens the usefulness and force of Christ's example,—He has, the scriptures say, left us *an example that we should follow his steps.* It was an example of blameless and perfect virtue; but he was, according to all opinions of him [n], qualified for

---

[n] This observation is applicable to the opinions concerning Christ which have hitherto been generally held by *Socinians*, who, in reality, make him more properly a *superior being* than a *man*, and differ from *Arians* chiefly by assigning, contrary to all that is credible, a different date to his existence.—Lately, some of them have lowered him into a man ignorant and peccable, and no way distinguished from the common men of his time except by being inspired; and this, I am sensible, by bringing him down more

to

for exhibiting it by high endowments which we do not poſſeſs, and communications of the ſpirit without meaſure which we cannot expect; and it is, on this account, leſs fitted to influence us. On other accounts, however, it is more forcible in proportion to his ſuperiority; and this is true, in particular, of his condeſcenſion, humility, meekneſs, and patience under ſufferings. The greater he was, the more we are obliged to admire theſe virtues in him; and the more we muſt be incited to practiſe them.—But there is one part of his example which, being founded on his pre-exiſtent dignity, is loſt entirely in the Socinian ſcheme. I mean; his quitting that dignity, and degrading himſelf to the condition of a mortal man in order to ſave men. This is an inſtance of benevolence to which we can

con-

to our own level, makes his example, in ſome reſpects, more an encouragement to us, and more fit to be propoſed to our imitation. See the note in page 133.

conceive no parallel; which is probably the admiration of angels; and which (were it duly believed and attended to) would make us incapable of not being ourselves examples of condefcenfion and benevolence. This is the part of Chrift's example which St. Paul has particularly recommended to our imitation in the paffage in *Phillippians* which I have already quoted. *Let this mind be in you which was alfo in Chrift Jefus; who, being in the form of God, did not affect to retain that form, but emptied himfelf of it, and took on him the form of a man and a fervant, and became obedient to death, even the death of the crofs Wherefore, God hath highly exalted him, and given him a name that is above every name, that at the name of Jefus every knee fhould bow and every tongue confefs that he is Lord, to the glory of God the Father.*—I reckon this one of the moft ftriking paffages in the New Teftament.—Let us comply with the exhortation delivered in it, and be always
ready

ready to spend and be spent in doing good, that we may rise as Christ rose.

I shall conclude with the following reflection.

If Christ was indeed possest of that superiority of nature which I have been asserting, how important must the service be which he came to perform. Would one so high have stooped so low to do only what a meaner agent might have done? I often feel myself deeply impressed by this consideration. The dignity of the *service*, and the dignity of the *agent*, imply and prove one another.—Think, Christians, how dreadful the danger must be which Christ left heaven to save you from; and neglect not so great a salvation. Remember that, at an expence greater than can be described, you have been raised to the hope of a resurrection from death to an endless life of ever-increasing happiness. Take care that you do not lose a benefit so transcendant, and sink at last

last into a death from which there will be no redemption. This cannot happen except through your own fault. But should it happen, Christ will not lose the fruits of his labour; for though *you* should have no share in them, *others* will, and myriads delivered by him from sin and death will hereafter unite in raising songs of praise and triumph, and ascribing blessing, and glory, and honour, and power to the *Lamb that was slain, and who hath redeemed us to God by his blood.*

SERMON V.

OF THE CHARACTER OF CHRIST AS THE SAVIOUR OF THE WORLD.

1 JOHN iv. 14.

We have seen, and do testify, that the Father sent the Son to be the Saviour of the world.

I HAVE thought it a proper part of the duty of my office in this place to give you a particular account of my ideas of that Gospel which we all profess, and on which we build our hopes of a future happy immortality. I have, already, proceeded a good way in the execution of this design. Before I proceed farther, I must desire

desire you to bear in mind as I go along, that, knowing how liable I am to error, I feel no disposition to be very anxious about bringing you over to my opinions. The rage for proselytism is one of the curses of the world. I wish to make no proselytes except to candour, and charity, and honest enquiry. You must judge for yourselves; and should any thing I *have* said in my former discourses, or *shall* say in the present discourse, give you any assistance in doing this, my principal end will be answered. I can, in this instance, as in most others, with much more confidence say what is *not*, than what *is* the truth. The *Athanasian* or *Calvinistic* scheme of Christianity I reject with strong conviction. The *Socinian* scheme also, on the two points which chiefly distinguish it, I find myself incapable of receiving. The reasons which determine my judgment on one of these points I have stated in my last discourse. I am now to state my my reasons for not receiving the *Socinian* doctrine on the other of these points.

God, my text says, SENT his SON to be the SAVIOUR OF THE WORLD.

I have observed that these words lead us to consider THREE particulars in the doctrine of our salvation by Christ.

First. The dignity of the Saviour. He was the SON OF GOD. This has been explained.

Secondly. The nature of the *instrumentality*, expressed by his having been SENT.

Thirdly. The nature of the service, expressed by his having been *sent* to be the SAVIOUR OF THE WORLD.

After I have said what I think necessary on the two last of these heads, you will be in full possession of my sentiments of the Gospel.

I am first of all to give you an account of the nature of that *instrumentality* in the
work

work of our redemption which is ascribed to Christ, when it is said that he was SENT of God to be the Saviour of the world. The following observations on this subject appear to me of some importance.

In the communication of benefits from one being to another there are two sorts of *instrumentality*. There is an instrumentality which (being constrained and passive) does not imply obligation to the instrument; and which, therefore, requires no gratitude except to the donor himself. And there is an instrumentality which (being spontaneous and active) *does* imply obligation to the instrument; and which, therefore, calls for gratitude to *him* as well as to the donor. Of the *former* sort is the instrumentality of a servant in conveying a benefit to another from his master. In this case, the servant being merely the conveyer, and having no choice with respect to the communication of the benefit, the person benefited carries

ries his views entirely to the master, and considers him alone as the cause of the benefit—Of the *latter* sort is the instrumentality of one employed by another as a *trustee* to distribute his bounty, but who, at the same time, is left at liberty, and may be unfaithful if he pleases. In this case, those who partake of the bounty feel obligation and gratitude to the *trustee* as well as to his principal. Room is left for the exercise of the free-will and discretion of the *trustee*; and the reception of the bounty is made to depend on his benevolence and honour in such a manner that, but for these, the recipient would have lost it.

Of this last sort is the instrumentality employed by the Deity in the distribution of his bounty among his reasonable creatures. He makes them, not passive instruments, but *trustees* and voluntary agents, in conveying to one another the blessings of his goodness. He makes them instruments in such a sense that the blessings received shall come from *them*, as well as primarily from *him*. He makes them, in short, *grantors* of benefits at the same time that they are *conveyers*. In no other way, could there have been room for gratitude to inferior beings for any benefits.

You must be sensible, that the principal blessings of our existence are not received by us immediately from the hands of the Deity. We see that he acts by instruments; by *passive* instruments in the material world; and by *voluntary* instruments in the intellectual world. In both, there is a series established of intermediate causes between us and that *Divine* power, wisdom, and goodness in which all causes terminate, on which they all depend, and to which ultimately they owe all their efficacy. Every reasonable and moral agent, placed in society and surrounded with fellow-creatures, is a *trustee* for distributing God's bounty. But, in the distribution, he is subjected to no restraints or limitations,
except

except such as his own prudence and virtue may prescribe to him. He has the option of being either slothful and treacherous, or diligent and faithful; and, consequently, of either with-holding happiness from his fellow-creatures, or granting it.—We have all of us *commissions* from God (as Christ had) to relieve distress, and to seek and to save that which is lost; and we should consider ourselves as *sent* of God for this purpose. These commissions have been given us, not by any specific orders or formal agreements, as among men (to conceive thus of even Christ's commission would, I doubt, be conceiving of the ways of God as too like our own ways) but by endowing us with powers to help our fellow-creatures, by planting within us kind affections promoting us to it, and by placing us in situations where we shall have opportunities for it. Beyond this we do not see that the Deity goes in making moral agents instruments of his goodness; nor was it fit that he should.—By constituting, in this manner, the plan of his universal government, he has given *consequence* to the agency of his reasonable creatures; for their agency would be of comparatively little consequence, were it employed merely in *carrying* benefits the enjoyment of which did not depend upon, and was not at all derived from, the beings who convey them.—In short; by the method of government of which I am endeavouring to give you an account, his creatures are made a kind of Deities to one another. They become *real* benefactors in the very same instances in which God is to be acknowledged as the *Supreme Benefactor*. Obligation to *them* takes place as well as to *him*; and, while our first gratitude is due to him (the cause of all causes) gratitude becomes due likewise to those inferior beings, on whose free-will and spontaneous instrumentality, he has been pleased to suspend the fruits of his beneficence.—There is, therefore, in this part

part of the conſtitution of nature unſpeakable wiſdom and goodneſs. Had nature been otherwiſe conſtituted; had no *abſolute* dependence of the ſtates of beings on one another been eſtabliſhed; were there in the univerſe no precariouſneſs of condition, no liableneſs to loſſes and calamities; were all the happineſs of beings aſcertained to them, independently of their own active choice and endeavours to bleſs one another.—Were *this* the plan of nature, the moral world would be little more than a kind of dead machinery. Moral agents would be incapable of doing any good to one another. No ſcope would be given to the exerciſe of benevolence; and, conſequently, all poſſibility of the greateſt happineſs would be excluded.

But to come nearer to the point I have in view.

I ſcarcely need tell you, that the inſtrumentality I aſcribe to Chriſt in the work of our redemption is of the kind I have laſt deſcribed. He was ſent of God to be the Saviour of the world in a manner that makes him (his benevolence) the cause of our salvation, as well as that original benevolence of the Deity from which all other benevolence is derived. He was the *Conveyer* of pardon and immortality to us, in such a sense that we owe them to *him*, as well as primarily to God.

This is a point of vast importance, and perhaps I may not be able sufficiently to explain it. I do not, however, think it attended with any peculiar difficulties; and if any one does, his difficulties must be owing to inattention and prejudice.— Were a good man, in the common course of life, to interpose, from principles of benevolence and pity, to save you from a calamity which, but for his exertions, would have ruined you; would you find any difficulty in reconciling your obligation to your deliverer to your obligation to the Deity? Though your benefactor was a free agent in delivering you, and though probably you would have been undone

but

but for his goodnefs; would you, on this account, think yourfelf lefs indebted to God's goodnefs? Would your feelings of gratitude to him interfere at all with your feelings of gratitude to the Deity? Would you not fay properly, that it was God put it into his heart to help you; and that it was he fent him and provided him for you? Would you not confider him as God's inftrument; and would not this (while it left you under the full impreffion of gratitude to God) improve and heighten your gratitude to your friend?—Suppofing then the truth to be, that Chrift is the author of our falvation in a way fimilar to this; that is, fuppofing that, by a voluntary interpofition from obedience to God and benevolence to man, he has delivered us from calamities ᵃ under which we might have perifh-

---

ᵃ " God gave his Son in the fame way of goodnefs to the world, as he affords particular perfons
" the

perished; and that he condescended to be born and to suffer and die, not merely to *convey*, in the sense first explained, blessings to us, but likewise to *obtain* them; supposing, I say, this to be the truth, no objection to it can be drawn from the necessity of acknowledging the goodness of God in all our benefits, and ascribing to him the glory of them.

Let us, therefore, in the next place enquire whether there is sufficient reason for believing this.

It

" the friendly assistance of their fellow-creatures, when, without it, their temporal ruin would be the certain consequence of their follies: In the same way of goodness, I say; though in a transcendent and infinitely higher degree. And the Son of God *loved us and gave himself for us*, with a love which he himself compares to that of human friendship: though in this case, all comparisons must fall infinitely short of the thing intended to be illustrated by them." Bishop Butler's Analogy of Religion natural and revealed to the constitution and course of nature, Part ii. ch. v. sec. 5.

It appears from what has been already said, that this enquiry is the same with the enquiry whether Christ is a *real* Saviour or not. For if he only *announces* salvation to us; if, properly speaking, he *obtains* nothing for us; if no extraordinary blessings were suspended on his benevolence, and we receive nothing on his account which we should not have otherwise equally had from God's goodness; if this is the truth, the importance of Christ as a Saviour is in a great degree lost, and, instead of viewing him in the light of the Restorer of a world consigned to the grave and the cause of eternal happiness to it, we must view him in the lower light of a Teacher, an Example, and a Martyr. I am satisfied that, according to the Scripture account, we are to view him principally in the former of these lights.

Before I enter on the proof of this, it is necessary I should take notice of that distrest state of mankind which it supposes, and

and of the need in which they might stand of a Saviour. The whole Christian scheme is founded on the supposition of a calamity in which our race had been involved, and which has been generally termed the FALL of man. What the true and full account of this event is, it is probably impossible for us to discover, or even to understand were it communicated to us. It is recorded in the third chapter of Genesis, but in a manner so mixed with emblems (derived, perhaps, from the ancient hieroglyphical manner of writing) and consequently so veiled and obscure, that I think little more can be learnt from it, than that there was a transaction, at the origin of our race and the commencement of this world, which degraded us to our present state, and subjected us to death and all its concomitant evils.—The credibility of such events in the creation cannot reasonably be denied. We see, in what falls under our notice of the Divine government, that in consequence

quence of the connexions which have been established and the powers given to beings, events are often happening which involve, not only individuals, but states and kingdoms in calamity.—What numbers of beings are there who are continually entering upon existence and happiness in this world, but by various causes are cut off and perish? What numbers of individuals are there among mankind who have lost valuable privileges, and are reduced to want and disease after enjoying health and affluence? How many kingdoms, once happy in the possession of peace, plenty, and liberty, have been plundered and ravaged, and at last conquered and ruined by savage oppressors and tyrants? Why should it be thought impossible, that even a *whole species* should also sometimes fall into calamity, and lose valuable blessings? What reasons can there be for expecting, that *orders* of beings should have their advantages absolutely secured to them, which will not like-

likewife apply to individuals and to communities?—In the latter cafe, our fenfes demonftrate fuch an expectation to be unreafonable. Should not this lead us to conclude, that it may be fo likewife in the former cafe?

The views of thofe perfons muft be very narrow who can imagine that the connexions among God's creatures extend no higher than man. Undoubtedly, man himfelf is connected with higher orders of beings, and fhould be confidered as only one link in a chain that reaches from inanimate matter to the Deity. And what revolutions [b], in particular circumftances and among particular beings, thefe

[b] The Scriptures feem to inform us of three great revolutions in the ftate of this habitable world.—Firft, the introduction of evil and of death among mankind, and a correfpondent change in external nature, by the FALL.—Secondly, an increafe of this evil, and a farther change in external nature by the DELUGE.—Thirdly, the deftruction of death, the renovation of nature, and the undoing of evil by the Meffiah at his future coming.

these connexions may produce, we cannot know. It is enough to know, that, whatever they are, and whatever the losses and sufferings may be which are sometimes occasioned by them, they are all under a perfect superintendency, and the result of a plan contrived in the best manner for bringing about the greatest possible happiness.—Such would be our wisest mode of reasoning did the light of revelation offer us no information. But you must be sensible that revelation has not been silent on this subject. It acquaints us, as has been just observed, that a calamity has happened to the human race; that we have suffered by our connexions under God's government; that we were made for immortality, but lost it and were brought down to our present sinful and mortal state. In Adam all have died. The sentence passed upon him has passed upon us all; *Dust thou art, and into dust thou shalt return.* By one man (St. Paul tells us) *sin entered into the world and death by by sin, and so death has passed upon all men.*—The appearances of the world, and the circumstances of our condition are such as make it very credible that our state may be a *fallen* state. We find ourselves in a situation where we are exposed to numberless temptations, and where the practice of virtue is often attended with great difficulties. We see that all mankind have sinned and come short of the glory of God[c]. There is no one who must not acknowledge himself a *guilty* being; who has not many transgressions to lament, and many inexcusable offences to repent of. Multitudes fall into atrocious vice.—May we not easily believe, that such

---

[c] " Whoever will consider the manifold miseries and extreme wickedness of the world, &c. will think he has little reason to object against the Scripture account that mankind is in a state of degradation, how difficult soever he may think it to account for, or even to form a distinct conception of the occasions and circumstances of it." See Bishop Butler's *Analogy*, &c. Part. ii. chap. 5.

such beings want a *Saviour?* A Saviour, not only to bring them to repentance and virtue, but to avert from them the confequences of paft guilt, and to render repentance itfelf available to happinefs?— This, however, is a point which has been much contefted by the favourers of Socinianifm. They maintain, that no Saviour could be wanted for this purpofe, the perfections of God requiring him to receive repenting finners. A return to virtue fuppofed, pardon and happinefs, they think, follow of courfe under the Divine government, whatever vice may have preceded it.—I cannot but think this a groundlefs affertion. It fuppofes, that the only end of punifhment is the reformation of the offender. But there is in vice an intrinfic demerit which (independently of [d] confequences) makes punifh-

[d] See a *Review of the principal Queftions and Difficulties in Morals*, chap. 5.

punishment proper; and it is rendered further proper by the necessity of vindicating the honour of God's broken laws, and of deterring beings who have *not* offended from wickedness. These are reasons for punishment which the reformation of the offender does not answer. And, in general, it seems fit, that in treating moral agents a regard should be had to what they *have* been, as well as to what they *are*; and that a distinction should be made between the cases of *innocents* and *penitents*, as well as between the cases of *penitents* and *impenitents*.—It is not, indeed, credible, that the connexion, established by the Divine laws between guilt and punishment, should be so easily broken as that every consequence of guilt should be immediately removed by repentance. This is contradicted by general and constant experience. When a person has lost a limb in a criminal pursuit, repentance will not restore it. When he has wasted his fortune or ruined his health by his

back.

vices, repentance will not bring them back. In such cases, remedies may be sometimes found, or the compassion of friends may relieve; but the mischief generally remains, notwithstanding any alteration of conduct.

With our condition as *sinful* and *guilty* is connected our condition as *mortal* creatures. These are the two circumstances in our condition which make it a *distress* condition. All men have corrupted their ways, and exposed themselves to the penalties annexed to guilt; and all men stand condemned to death. The Scriptures inform us that a deliverer from death was promised at the time it was introduced. *(The seed of the woman shall bruise the serpent's head,* Gen. iii. 15.) But this implies that, without a deliverer, we must have remained under the power of death, and consequently lost a future state. It seems a break in the thread of conscious existence, which cannot be usual in the transition of reasonable beings from lower to higher states. It is a *catastrophe* universally dreaded, threatening extinction, and bearing every appearance of being what the Scriptures make it, an *adventitious* evil [e] and not an *original* part of God's plan.

Such

---

[e] Some think the account in Genesis of the introduction of death to be an *Allegory* intended to teach not a FACT, but a MORAL LESSON; and, consequently, they think the present *mortal* state of man to be not an adventitious state, but that for which he was at first intended. Were this true, it would be necessary to look upon Christ's saving the world by delivering it from death, as an interposition to save it from the state for which it was made, and in which the Creator had placed it; and it is, I think, an argument in favour of Christianity, that, by grounding our redemption on a *fall*, it has led us to juster conceptions.

The following words in the Apochryphal book entitled the *Wisdom of Solomon,* are very remarkable. Chap. ii. 24. *God created man to be immortal. He made him to be an image of his own eternity. Nevertheless; through envy of the Devil, came death into the world; and they that hold of his side do find it.*—The interpretation, in these words of the account of the fall has been generally received by Jews and Christians; and it deserves

Such is the condition of man: A condition which, though it leaves abundant proofs of the wisdom and goodness of the Creator, shews us that we might have needed salvation. And it also shews us in what this salvation must consist. It appears, that it must consist in the deliverance of *guilty* creatures from the connexion established by the Divine laws between guilt and punishment; and in the deliverance of *mortal* creatures from death.

This, therefore, is the FIRST argument I would use to prove that Christ was

---

serves notice, that Christ has referred to it in the words (John viii. 44.) *The Devil was a murderer from the beginning;* and the apostle John in the words (1 John ii. 8.) *The Devil sinneth from the beginning. For this purpose the Son of God was manifested, that he might destroy the works of the Devil.* And in the Revelation, by calling Satan, the OLD SERPENT.—But the clearest reference to this interpretation is in the epistle to the Hebrews, chap. ii. 14. *Forasmuch as the children are partakers of flesh and blood, he also himself took part of the same; that, through death he might destroy him that had the power of death; that is, the devil; and deliver them who, through fear of death, were all their lifetime subject to bondage.*

a Saviour in a higher sense than by being a teacher. Our cases as *sinful* and *mortal* creatures required more than instruction. Instruction could only bring us to repentance. It could not make repentance the means of remission; or an exemption from the effects of guilt. It could not create a fitness that offenders should be favoured as if they had never offended. It could not raise from death, or restore to a new life.

I could, however, even allow all this; and still maintain that Christ was more than a teacher. For, granting the necessary availableness of repentance in all cases to favour and happiness, it may be asked to what *degree* of favour and happiness it is necessarily available? Must our imperfect virtue, a virtue preceded, perhaps, by atrocious wickedness as well as accompanied with numberless infirmities; must *such* virtue be entitled to *such* favour as Christianity promises, including in it, not only pardon and a remission of punishment,

ment, but a glorious *immortality*; an eternal exiſtence in ever-increaſing felicity and honour. If ſo, then indeed it will follow that we can owe no more to Chriſt than inſtruction.—But there cannot be a ſhadow of reaſon for ſuch an aſſertion. Even *ſinleſs* virtue can have no title to that ſuper-abundance of grace promiſed by Chriſtianity. It might then have been made precarious, and left to depend on a voluntary exertion of benevolence in our favour.

But the main evidence on this point muſt be taken from the Scriptures. I ſhould run this diſcourſe to an immoderate length, were I to attempt to give you any particular account of thoſe declarations of Scripture which might be here quoted.—Chriſt is ſtyled *the propitiation for our ſins. In him, we are told, we have redemption through his blood, even the forgiveneſs of our ſins. He made his life an offering for iniquity, ſhed his blood for the remiſſion of ſins, and appeared once in the end of the world for ever to put away ſin by the ſacrifice of himſelf.*—I cannot think that ſuch expreſſions ſignify only, that he died to ſeal the covenant of grace, and to aſſure us of pardon. Their obvious meaning ſeems to be, that, as the ſacrifices under the law of Moſes expiated guilt and procured remiſſion, ſo Chriſt's ſhedding his blood and offering up his life was the means of remiſſion and favour to penitent ſinners.—But the declarations of moſt conſequence, are thoſe which acquaint us that Chriſt came *that we might have life, and that we might have it more abundantly.—That he laid down his life for the life of the world.—That he is that eternal life which was with the Father.—That by death he deſtroyed death; and that, as by Adam came ſin and death, ſo by Chriſt ſhall come the reſurrection of the dead, and grace reign through righteouſneſs unto eternal life.* The New Teſtament is full of language to this purpoſe.—And, ſurely,

it

it signifies that he is more than a *prophet* and *reformer*. It sets him before us as the Author of life to a race obnoxious to punishment and devoted to death; as their Deliverer from the grave, and the Restorer of a distrest world. It implies that our resurrection from death to an endless life depended on his interposition; and that by uniting himself to our nature, passing through human life, and suffering and dying as he did, he acquired the power of making us happy for ever.—*Having been made perfect through sufferings, he became the Author of eternal salvation to all that obey him. He died for us that whether we sleep or wake we should live with him.* Eternal life is the gift of God through him—through him not merely as the *Revealer*; but likewise as the *Dispenser* [f], and (under God) the *Procurer* of it.

Thirdly,

---

[f] It is universally agreed among Christians, that the power of *dispensing* to penitent sinners the blessings of

Thirdly. I would defire you to confider that Chrift is called the Saviour of the WORLD; that is, of ALL MANKIND; and that he could not be fo merely as a *prophet* and

of the Chriftian covenant (that is, pardon and immortality) is a part of the reward of Chrift's fervices and merit. And it was, indeed, a reward worthy of them if *his* difpenfing them, in confequence of his obedience to death, was, like all that we fee of God's government, the means and the condition of the enjoyment of them: And, I have no doubt, but this was chiefly *the joy fet before him for which he endured the crofs defpifing the fhame,* Heb. xii. 2. But if thefe were bleffings which had not been loft; which could not be withheld without a violation of the Divine perfections; and which, therefore, penitent and virtuous men would have equally enjoyed *with* or *without* Chrift; the fervice, the merit, and the reward all vanifh. Mankind wanted only to be inftructed and brought to repentance; and Chrift, being fimply a man, was equal to no higher fervice.

It deferves particular confideration here, that none who think a future ftate not to be difcoverable by the light of nature, can think that human virtue gives a claim to a future immortality; for, on this fuppofition, there would be the fame reafon for expecting a future im-

and a *reformer*. In these capacities, he can be the Saviour only of those who receive his instructions, and to whom the influence of his Gospel has reached; and consequently, all virtuous men *before* his coming, and all virtuous Heathens *since* his coming can owe nothing to him. But the language of Scripture is, that he *tasted death for every man*.—That the benefits he has obtained extend as far as the effects of Adam's fall.—And that by his obedience, *the free gift came upon all men to justification of life*.

Fourthly.

immortality that there is for believing the moral perfections of the Deity. But this is far from being the opinion of those who hold the *Socinian* doctrine. On the contrary; Dr. PRIESTLEY asserts, that all the appearances of nature are against a future state ; and, that the evidence for it rests solely on the mission and resurrection of Jesus Christ. I cannot concur with Dr. Priestley in this opinion ; but were it right, there would be no room for doubting whether (agreeably to the Scripture account) immortality is a blessing which *may* have been lost and afterwards regained through the redemption that is in Christ.

Fourthly. It deserves your consideration, that the superiority of Christ's nature evidently implies, that he came to perform a service which no mere man could perform; and, therefore, greater than any service consisting only in enlightening and reforming the world. The dignity of the agent and the dignity of the service prove one another, as I observed in my former discourse.

Admit that Christ was indeed the *Life* as well as the *Light* of the world.—Admit that he was not only the *Revealer* and *Conveyer*, but the *Obtainer* of pardon and immortality to mankind.—And a service will appear transcendent and unspeakable, adequate to that stupendous humiliation which was the means of it, and worthy of the interposition of that MESSIAH who was in the beginning with God.

But suppose that he came to do no more than a *man* could do—suppose that for no higher service, he was so greatly rewarded as to have a *name given him that is above every*

every name, not only in this world but in that which is to come, angels, authorities, and powers being made subject to him.—And the consequence will be introducing a disproportion between the means and the end, (between Christ's service and his reward) which is entirely incomprehensible and incredible.

Let me farther ask. In what; according to the doctrine I am opposing, consisted that love of Christ which PASSES KNOWLEDGE mentioned by St. Paul; and that scheme of redemption into which he represents angels as stooping to look? The one is sunk down to a love that men have exercised; and the other into a scheme for teaching and reforming mankind that men could carry on.

This leads me to desire you to consider fifthly; that, according to this doctrine, Christ was a *Saviour* in no higher sense than that in which the Apostles, or any other useful teachers of religion, may be so called. But would not the apostles have

have been shocked at any such ideas of them. St. Paul asks the Corinthians—*Was Paul crucified for you?* Plainly implying, that it was not possible for him to be crucified for them in any sense like that in which Christ was crucified for them.— In like manner, had he been called the *Saviour of the World* as Christ was, on account of what he did and endured to teach and reform the world; he would probably have replied with indignation—" Did " Paul die for the sins of the world?" " Will Paul raise the world from the " dead?"

Once more I would observe to you on this subject (as I did in my former discourse on the subject of Christ's dignity) that the prejudices against the doctrine I am defending are derived in a great degree from inattention to the nature and the extent of the connexions and dependencies which take place in the creation. The plan of the Deity in governing

ing his creatures is to suspend their participation of his bounty on their agency, and to make their spontaneous instrumentality the channel and the condition of the communication of the fruits of his goodness.—This is, certainly, the plan which all we see of the Divine government exhibits; and it should be carefully remembered, that what we see is in this case the best clue we can use in our enquiries, and that we cannot go upon safer ground than when we judge that part of the Divine government which extends *above* man to be analogous to that part of it which lies *before* us.

It is here, I think, remarkable, that we are able to discover that the plan thus exhibited to our view is the best plan, because it gives scope and weight to the agency of intelligent beings, and makes them capable of being useful to one another, and, therefore, of enjoying that happiness which assimilates them most to the Deity.—I have made some of these ob-

obfervations at the beginning of this difcourfe; but they are of fo much importance, that they can hardly be repeated too often.—Had there been no poffibility of loffes and fufferings in the creation; had all beings and all orders of beings ftood fingle and unconnected; and had their privileges been fecured to them without depending on either their own exertions or the exertions of other beings—had this been the plan of God's government, this world would have loft its value and dignity. It would have been a world without room in it for generofity, for gratitude, for great atchievements, and all the fublimeft joys that can be felt by a reafonable creature. —Had, in particular, that fyftem of orders of beings in which probably man is a link been thus conftituted, that MESSIAH revealed by Chriftianity could have known nothing of the joy for which he endured the crofs. He muft have been a ftranger to the fatisfaction he felt when he faw of the travail of his foul; and he muft have

loft

loft that addition to *his* happiness which he has derived from promoting *our* happiness.

It is high time to relieve you from your attention to this important subject. In delivering my sentiments upon it I have said nothing of *substitution,* or *satisfaction,* or any of those explanations of the manner of our redemption by Christ which have been given by Divines. Some of these explanations are in the highest degree absurd, and I receive none of them, thinking that the Scriptures have only revealed to us the fact that *God sent his Son to be the Saviour of the World,* and chusing to satisfy myself with those ideas respecting it which I have laid before you[g].

Per-

---

[g] " Some have endeavoured to explain the efficacy of what Christ has done and suffered for us beyond what the Scripture has authorized. Others, probably, because they could not explain it, have been for taking it away, and confining his office
" as

Perhaps some of these ideas are wrong; and, should that be the case, I am under no apprehensions of any ill consequences, being

"as Redeemer of the world to his instruction, ex-
"ample, and government of the Church. Whereas
"the doctrine of the Gospel appears to be, not only
"that he taught the efficacy of repentance, but ren-
"dered it of the efficacy which it is by what he did
"and suffered for us; that he obtained for us the
"benefit of having our repentance accepted to eter-
"nal life, &c. How, and in what particular way
"it had this efficacy, there are not wanting persons
"who have endeavoured to explain; but I do not
"find that the Scriptures have explained it. It is
"our wisdom thankfully to accept the benefit with-
"out disputing how it was procured."——Bishop Butler's *Analogy of Religion natural and revealed to the constitution and course of nature,* Part ii. chap. 5.

"Let reason be kept to, and if any part of the
"Scripture account of the redemption of the world
"by Christ can be shewn to be really contrary to it,
"let the Scripture, in the name of God, be given
"up. But let not such poor creatures as we go on
"objecting to an infinite scheme that we do not see
"the necessity or usefulness of all its parts, and call
"this reasoning." *Ib.*

being perfuaded that my intereſt in this redemption depends not on the juſtneſs of my conceptions of it, or the rectitude of my judgment concerning it, but on the ſincerity of my heart.—Indeed, I ſeldom feel much of that ſatisfaction which ſome derive from being ſure they have found out truth. But I derive great comfort from believing, that error, when involuntary, is innocent; and that all that is required of me, as a condition of acceptance, is faithfully endeavouring to find out and to practiſe truth and right.

I will conclude with exhorting you

Firſt, to make it your ſtudy, by a holy life, to ſecure an intereſt in this ſalvation. —We ſhould be often putting to ourſelves the queſtion in Heb. ii. 3. *How ſhall we eſcape if we neglect ſo great a ſalvation?*—A great ſalvation is wrought out for us and offered us; but it is only *offered* us. We cannot be made actual partakers

takers of it without the concurrence of our own wills and endeavours. We do not fee, in any cafe, that it is God's plan to *force* any one to be happy. The impenitent and vicious are incapable of happinefs.—Let us then forfake every evil way, and practife univerfal righteoufnefs. There is no motive to this, which ftrikes my mind more ftrongly, than the reflexion on the vaftnefs of the danger implied in the vaftnefs of the *apparatus* for faving us. How fhocking will be our fate fhould any of us after all remain unfaved; and find that Chrift lived and died in vain, as to any benefit we fhall derive from him?— I am fenfible that there are fome very wife and good Chriftians who think this cannot be the cafe ultimately with any human being; and that even the impenitent will (after a feverity of future punifhment proportioned to the different degrees of guilt) be recovered to virtue and happinefs; and thus Chrift's triumph over fin and death become at laft univerfal

fal and complete.—This is an opinion which the feelings of every benevolent man would determine him eagerly to embrace, could it be fhewn to be confiftent with the language of Scripture; and I dare not pronounce that it is not fo. But God forbid, that any of us fhould rifk upon it the *exiftence* of our immortal fouls; or fuffer fuch an expectation to render us lefs fearful of the confequences of vice. Our Saviour has declared (and it is one of the moft awful declarations in the Bible) that *the hour is coming when all that are in their graves fhall hear the voice of the Son of Man, and fhall come forth. They who have done good to the refurrection of life; but they who have done evil to the refurrection of damnation,* John v. 29.—What this DAMNATION will be, and in what it will terminate, is at prefent unknown and inconceivable. The Scriptures lead us to think of it as a *fecond* death more terrible than the prefent, and fometimes call it *everlafting* deftruction, struction, and compare it to a fire which burns up and confumes what is thrown into it. The bare *poſſibility* that thefe expreſſions fignify total extermination is frightful; and ſhould be fufficient to deter effectually from wickednefs. And if it does not, there is reafon to believe that no *certainty* of fuch a puniſhment would have a much greater effect.

Secondly, Let us, as far as we are confcious of having returned to our duty, rely on Chrift as our Saviour; and rejoice in the hope of eternal life through him. We may confider him as addreſſing us as he did his apoſtles in John xiv. 1. *Let not your hearts be troubled. You believe in God. Believe alfo in me.* He is that word of God and great Meſſiah, who was made fleſh and dwelt among us to blefs us with light, inftruction, pardon, and immortality; and it will be inexcufable not to carry about with us a deep fenfe of our obligations to him, and to honour and love him. But,

Thirdly,

Thirdly, While we do this, let us take care not to overlook that firſt cauſe and giver of all good to whoſe antecedent love we owe Jeſus Chriſt. This is an admonition of the laſt conſequence; and you muſt not be diſpleaſed with me for taking every occaſion to inculcate it. Mankind have always been too prone to pay undue honours to inferior benefactors, and to terminate their views in *ſecond* cauſes. It is this that has produced that baſe idolatry which in all ages has diſgraced the world, and led even Chriſtians to worſhip the creature rather than the Creator. Let us ſtudy to be wiſer. Let us, in the bleſſings of redemption as well as all our other bleſſings, learn to center our views in God, and fly from every form of public devotion that has any other object than that ONE Being *of whom, and through whom, and to whom are all things.*—We ſhould honour Chriſt ardently as our Lord and Saviour; but we ſhould honour him as having *the ſame God and Father with ourſelves,*

selves, and never think of any thing so absurd and shocking as elevating *him* who was sent to an equality with the self-existent Being who sent him.

Lastly, The doctrine on which I have insisted has a tendency to console us under the troubles of life ; and, particularly[h], under the distresses arising from the havock which death is making continually among our friends. Christ rose from the dead as the *first-fruits of them that sleep.* He has assured us that since he lives, we shall live also. Had we not been blest with this information, our prospect in circumstances of sorrow would have been discouraging. We should have looked forward to death, not (as we now may) with hope and triumph, but with doubt and

---

[h] What follows was occasioned by the death of one of the principal members of the society to which these discourses were addressed ; and by the attendance of his family, the first time after his death, on the morning when this discourse was delivered.

and anxiety; and this king of terrors, inftead of appearing a friend and a deliverer, would have appeared an enemy and deftroyer. Happy then is the lot of every true Chriftian. His religion kindles for him a bright light in this benighted world, and enables him to defcry beyond the grave a better world, and millions in it raifed to honour and blifs, and uniting in taking up St. Paul's fong of triumph—*Oh! death where is thy fting? Oh! grave where is thy victory? Thanks be to God who giveth us the victory through our Lord Jefus Chrift.*

The apprehenfion of our liablenefs to fuch fufferings as fometimes attend a dying illnefs (and as the friend went through for whom fome of us now appear in mourning) has a tendency to deject us. But we ought not defpond. All is wifely ordered, and all will end well. While waiting for our laft conflict, we fhould ftudy to keep our minds undifturbed, committing our exiftence to him who gave it, it, resolving not to feel pain till it comes, attending to nothing anxiously but our duty, and looking forward with joyful hope to that period when, at the call of the Saviour of the world, we shall spring up from the dust, and draw immortal breath, in those new heavens and that new earth where all the virtuous are to meet and never more to feel pain or sorrow. *Wherefore let us comfort one another with these words.*

SERMON VI.

OF THE SECURITY OF A VIRTUOUS COURSE.

PROVERBS X. 9.

He that walketh uprightly, walketh surely.

THESE words express one of the most important of all maxims. They tell us, that in the practice of virtue there is SAFETY. Much higher praise may be bestowed upon it. We may say that with it are connected peace, honour, dignity, the favour of God, happiness *now*, and ETERNAL happiness *hereafter*: And we have reason enough to think this true. But whether true or not, it is is at least true, that there is SAFETY in it.

Christianity informs us, that good men will be raised from death to enjoy a glorious immortality, through that Saviour of the world who tasted death for every man. But let the evidence for this be supposed precarious and unsatisfactory.—Let it be reckoned uncertain whether a virtuous course will terminate in such infinite blessings under the Divine government as Christians are taught to expect.—Still there will remain sufficient evidence to prove, that in all events it must be the *safest*, and therefore our *wisest* course.

I cannot better employ the present time than in endeavouring to explain and illustrate this truth. But previously to this, it will not be amiss to make a few observations on the character of the man who walks uprightly.

Uprightness signifies the same with integrity or sincerity. It implies a freedom from

from guile and the faithful difcharge of every known duty. An upright man allows himfelf in nothing that is inconfiftent with truth and right. He complies with all the obligations he is under, and avoids every kind of prevarication and falfehood. He maintains an equal and uniform regard to the whole of righteoufnefs. He hates alike all fin, and practifes every part of virtue, from an unfeigned attachment to it eftablifhed in his foul. This is what is moft effential to the character of an upright man. He is governed by no finifter ends, or indirect views, in the difcharge of his duty. It is not the love of fame, or the defire of private advantages, or mere natural temper that produces his virtuous conduct; but an affection to virtue *as* virtue; a fenfe of the weight and excellence of the obligations of righteoufnefs; and a zeal for the honour of God and the happinefs of mankind. But to be a little more particular.

Uprightnefs of character comprehends in it right conduct with refpect to God, and man, and ourfelves.—The perfon I am defcribing is firft of all upright in all his tranfactions with GOD. His religion is not an hypocritical fhew and oftentation. He *is* that which he *appears* to be to his fellow-creatures. His religious acts are emanations from a heart full of piety. He makes confcience of *private* as well as *public* devotion, and endeavours to walk blamelefsly in all God's ordinances. He attends on religious fervices not to be feen of men; but from a fenfe of duty and gratitude to his Maker; and, inftead of making them a cover for bad defigns, or compenfations for immorality, he makes them incentives to the difcharge of all moral duties, and the means of rendering him more benevolent, amiable, and worthy.

Again. Uprightnefs implies faithfulnefs in all our tranfactions with *ourfelves*. It is very common for men to impofe upon

upon themselves; to wink at offensive truths; and to practise unfair arts with their own minds. This is entirely inconsistent with the character of an upright man. He endeavours to be faithful to himself in all that he thinks and does, and to divest his mind of all unreasonable biasses. He is fair and honest in all his enquiries and deliberations, ready to own his mistakes, and thankful for every help to discover them. He wishes to know nothing but what is true, and to *practise* nothing but what is right. He is open to conviction, indifferent where he finds truth, and prepared to follow it wherever it can lead him. He is often disciplining his heart, searching into the principles of conduct within him, and labouring to detect his faults in order to rectify them.

Further. Uprightness includes in it candour, fairness, and honesty in all our transactions with our *fellow-creatures*. An upright man may be depended upon in all his

his profeſſions and engagements. He never, in any affair, goes beyond the limits of juſtice and equity. He never deceives or over-reaches. He is true to his promiſes, and faithful to every truſt repoſed in him. All his gains are the gains of virtuous induſtry. All falſehood and lies, all low cunning and fraudulent practiſes are his abhorrence.—In ſhort; he maintains a ſtrict regard to veracity in his words, and to honour in his dealings. He adheres ſteadfaſtly in all circumſtances to what he judges to be righteſt and beſt; and were it poſſible for you to look thro' his ſoul, you would ſee the love of goodneſs predominant within him. You would ſee benevolence and piety governing his thoughts. You would ſee him, within the incloſure of his own breaſt, as honeſt and worthy as he is on the open ſtage of the world.

Such is the character of the man who walks uprightly. I am next to ſhew you how *ſurely* he walks.

In

In order to acquire a juſt notion of this, it is proper we ſhould take into conſideration, firſt, the ſafety which ſuch a perſon enjoys with reſpect to the happineſs of the preſent life. Nothing is plainer than that, if we regard only our temporal intereſt, an upright courſe is the ſafeſt courſe. In order to be ſenſible of this, you ſhould think of the troubles which men very often bring upon themſelves by deviating from integrity. It is very difficult to go on for any time in diſhoneſty and falſehood, without falling into perplexity and diſtreſs. A man in ſuch a courſe ſuſpects every body, and is ſuſpected by every body He wants the love and eſteem of his fellow-creatures. He is obliged to be continually on his guard, and to uſe arts to evade law and juſtice. He walks in the dark along a crooked path full of ſnares and pits.—On the contrary. The path of uprightneſs is ſtrait and broad. It is ſmooth, open, and eaſy. He that walks in it walks in the light,

and

and may go on with resolution and confidence, inviting rather than avoiding the inspection of his fellow-creatures. He is apprehensive of no dangers. He is afraid of no detection. He is liable to none of the causes of shame and disgrace. It is an advantage to him to be observed and watched. The more narrowly his conduct is examined, the more he will be loved and respected.

A person, for instance, who, in the affairs of trade, deviates from truth and honour, is likely to sink into great calamities. Want, and trouble, and infamy often prove his lot. Most of us have been witnesses of this. How many instances are there of persons who, forsaking the plain path of uprightness, have entangled themselves beyond the possibility of being extricated, and involved their families in the deepest misery; but who, probably, had they been honest, would have escaped every difficulty, and passed through life easily and happily. We know

know not, indeed, what we do when we turn aside from virtue and righteousness. Such a train of consequences may follow as will issue in the loss of all that is valuable. It is past doubt, that, in every profession and calling, the way of uprightness is the most free from perplexity. It is ths way of peace and satisfaction. He that keeps in it will at least avoid the pain of a reproaching conscience. He is sure of enjoying his own approbation; and it may be expected that his worldly affairs will go on smoothly, quietly, and comfortably.

This puts me in mind of desiring you to consider particularly, that an upright conduct is commonly the most sure way to obtain success in our worldly concerns. You will observe, that I say it is the most *sure* way; not that it is the *shortest*. There are many more *expeditious* ways of getting money and acquiring fortunes. He that will violate the rules of justice, or break the laws of his country, or not scruple to

take

take false oaths, may easily get the start of an upright man, and rise in a little time to wealth and preferment. It is often in a man's power, by a base action, to introduce himself at once into ease and plenty. But wretched are those men who secure any worldly advantages by such methods. There is a canker at the root of their successes and riches. What they gain is unspeakably less than what they lose. It is attended with inward anguish, with the curse of heaven, and inconceivable future danger.—But though it must be thus acknowledged, that there are *shorter* ways to profit and success than by walking uprightly, there are certainly none so *sure*. Universal experience has proved that (agreeably to a common and excellent maxim) " honesty is the best policy." It may be slow in its operation; and, for this reason, many persons have not patience enough for it. But it is in the end generally certain. An upright man must recommend himself by

degrees

degrees to all that know him. He has always the greateſt credit, and the moſt unembarraſſed affairs. There are none who are not difpoſed to place a confidence in him, and who do not chuſe to deal with him. The difadvantages, therefore, already mentioned, under which he labours, are counterbalanced by many great advantages. He may not be able to thrive ſo faſt, nor perhaps ſo *much* as others. He is obliged to deny himſelf the gains which others make by the wrong practices common in their trade; and, on this account, he may be under a neceſſity of contenting himſelf with ſmall gains. But it muſt be conſidered, that he can ſeldom fail of a tolerable ſubſiſtence, attended with comfort and the trueſt enjoyment of himſelf. Though his gains may be ſmall, they are always ſweet. He has with them an eaſy conſcience, the bleſſing of God, and ſecurity againſt numberleſs grievous evils. And the ſmalleſt gains of this ſort are infinitely preferable to the greatest gains that can be obtained by wrong methods.

Thus you see that, with respect to our interest in *this* world, he that walketh uprightly walketh surely.—Let us next consider the security which an upright conduct gives with respect to *another* world.

After this life is over we are to enter on another world. The most sceptical principles give us no sufficient reason for denying this. Whatever may be true of the order and administration of nature, it must be *possible* that there should be a future state. And, if there is, it is highly probable, that it will be a state of much greater extent and longer duration than the present. Nothing, therefore, can be of more consequence to us than to know by what means we may secure the best condition and the greatest safety in it: And it is not possible to doubt, but the practise of religious goodness is the proper means to be used for this purpose. If

If any thing is clear, it is so, that the upright and the worthy, in all events, and through every period of duration, must stand the best chance for escaping misery and obtaining happiness.—That our happiness hereafter may depend on our conduct here is certain, because we find, in the present state, that the happiness of every successive period of human life is made to depend, in a great measure, on our conduct in the preceding periods. The happiness of mature life depends on the habits acquired and the pains taken in early life; and mature life spent in folly and vice generally makes a miserable old age. It is, therefore, very credible that a virtuous conduct may have an effect on our condition hereafter.—No one, indeed, can well carry infidelity so far as to deny, that, if there is a future state, it is likely that the righteous will fare better in it than the wicked. All we observe of the government of the Deity, and all that we can learn with respect to his character, leads us to believe that he muſt approve righteouſneſs and hate wickedneſs: And, in the ſame proportion that he does this, he muſt favour the one and diſcountenance the other. We ſee, in what lies before us of the conſtitution of the world, many great evils annexed to wickedneſs; and many great bleſſings annexed to righteouſneſs; and we ſee, likewiſe, in the one an eſſential tendency to produce univerſal evil, and in the other an eſſential tendency to produce univerſal good. This demonſtrates to us the holy diſpoſition of the Author of nature; and what we ought to reckon upon is, that he will manifeſt this diſpoſition more and more; and that the ſcheme of moral government now begun will be hereafter completed.—To act righteouſly is to act like God. It is to promote the order of his creation. It is to go into his conſtitution of nature. It is to follow that conſcience which he has given us to be the guide of our conduct. It muſt, therefore,

fore, be the likelieſt way to arrive at happineſs, and to guard againſt miſery under his government. The accountableneſs of our natures, and our neceſſary perceptions of excellence and good deſert in virtue, demonſtrate this; nor is it at all conceivable, that we do not go upon ſure grounds when we draw this concluſion. —But there is much more to be here ſaid. There are many reaſons which prove, that the neglect of virtue may be followed by a dreadful puniſhment hereafter. The preſages of conſcience; the concurring voice of mankind in all ages; our unavoidable apprehenſions of ill-deſert in vice; and the diſtreſſes now produced by it, are enough to lead us to expect this. The Chriſtian religion confirms this expectation in a manner the moſt awful, by teaching us that the *wicked ſhall be turned into hell with all that forget God*; that they ſhall be excluded from the ſociety of wiſe and good beings; and puniſhed *with everlaſting deſtruction from the preſence of the Lord*

Lord and the glory of his power. It is, at least, possible this may be the truth. The arguments for a righteous government in nature, and for the truth of Christianity, have at least force enough to prove that it is not certain but that wickedness will produce the greatest losses and evils in another world; and that, consequently, there is a real and inconceivable danger attending it.—Consider, now, that an upright life is a sure preservative from this danger. If all who forget God and practise iniquity are hereafter to be rejected by the Deity, and to be consigned to *everlasting destruction*; if, I say, this should prove to be the truth, the good man will be safe and the wicked man undone. But should all that reason and Christianity teach us on this point prove a delusion; still a good man will *lose* nothing, and a bad man will *get* nothing. Nay, a good man, even in this case, will gain a great deal: For he will gain all that satisfaction which goodness
gene-

generally brings with it in this life, and which vice muſt want.

Thus you fee what fecurity an upright man enjoys. He goes upon even and firm ground. He has on his fide all good beings; the convictions of his confcience; the order of nature; and the power of the Deity. It is impoſſible he ſhould be deceived in thinking, that it is right to adhere inviolably to the laws of righteouſneſs. Should there be that execution of Divine juſtice on wickedneſs which we have been taught to expect, he will have nothing to fear. The *worſt* that can happen to him is better than the *beſt* that may happen to an unrighteous man. The *beſt* that wicked men generally expect is the loſs of exiſtence at death; and this is the *worſt* that can happen to a good man. But upon the one, it will come after a life of ſhame, and diſeaſe, and folly; and on the other like ſleep at night after a day ſpent in peace, and health, and honour, and uſe-
ful

ful labour.—I need not tell you what a recommendation this is of a courſe of uprightneſs.—It is our fureſt guard in all events: our beſt ſhelter againſt evils under God's government. Safety is what every perſon, in the common concerns of life, values and ſeeks. Here alone is it to be found completely and certainly. Nothing but virtuous conduct can preſerve us from the danger of God's difpleaſure, and of ruin after death. Without it we muſt ſtand expoſed to the fevereſt calamities that can come upon reaſonable beings.

I will conclude this difcourſe with the following inferences.

Firſt, From all I have ſaid we learn, in the plaineſt manner, how much we are bound in prudence to walk uprightly. This appears to be prudent if we regard only our preſent intereſt. The way in which an upright man walks (it has been ſhewn) is plain and open. It is ſo eaſy to find

find it, that we can never swerve from it while we retain an honest desire to keep in it. It is liable to no hazards; and it is always pleasant and joyous. More *compendious* ways, I have acknowledged, we may sometimes find to wealth and power; but they are full of danger, and he who forsakes integrity in order to go into them, and thus by a short cut to get at worldly advantages, acts like a man who forsakes a quiet and sure path in order to run the risk of being lost among quicksands, or of breaking his neck by going over rocks and precipices. If, therefore, we love prudence, we shall not, in our temporal concerns, ever swerve from uprightness.

But we have reason to apprehend that we shall exist in another state; and if we consider this, we shall be forced to conclude from what has been said, that the prudence of a virtuous course is greater than can be expressed. If this life is not our whole existence, some precautions ought

ought to be used with respect to the state that is to succeed it; and the best precaution is the practise of true piety and goodness. If there is a life to come, it will, in all probability, be a state of retribution, where present inequalities will be set right, and the vicious sink into infamy and misery. The practise of virtue is, in this case, our security. It is the image of the Deity in our souls; and what we ought to reckon upon is, that nothing amiss will ever happen to it. Let us then adhere to it in all events. Let us endeavour, in this instance, to use the same prudence that the children of the world use in *their* affairs. What pains will they take, and what precautions will they employ, to avoid any dangers which they foresee, or to prevent evils which may possibly come upon them?—There is a danger hanging over us, as moral agents, greater than any this world can threaten us with; a danger dreadful and unutterable; the danger of falling into the punishment

nishment of sin, and of losing eternal happiness. Were there ever so hard and expensive a method proposed to us of being secured against this danger, it would be our wisdom chearfully to practise it.—But true goodness affords us, not a hard and expensive, but a cheap and easy method of being secured against it. Walking uprightly will add to our *present* comfort, at the same time that it will preserve us from *future* danger. What is required of us, in this instance, is only to part with our follies and diseases; and to make ourselves happy *now*, in order to be safe *for ever*.

All I have been saying is true, though there should be the greatest uncertainty with respect to the principles of religion. I have been all along speaking on the supposition of such an uncertainty, in order to set before you, in a stronger light, the wisdom of being virtuous, and the folly of a sinful course.—But if we will suppose that there is no such uncertainty: If we will

will suppose it not only possible, but probable or morally certain, that the principles of religion are true; that Christianity comes from God; and that, agreeably to its assurances, all who are now in their graves shall hereafter *hear the voice of the Son of God, and come forth; those who have done good to the resurrection of life, and those who have done evil to the resurrection of damnation:* If, I say, we suppose this to be the truth, how great will the wisdom of a virtuous course appear, and how shocking the folly of wickedness?

There are, probably, few speculative and enquiring men who do not sometimes find themselves in a state of dejection, which takes from them much of the satisfaction arising from their faith in very important and interesting truths. Happy, indeed, is the person who enjoys a flow of spirits so even and constant as never to have experienced this. Of myself I must say, that I have been far from being

being so happy. Doubts and difficulties have often perplexed me, and thrown a cloud over truths which, in the general course of my life, are my support and consolation. There are, however, many truths, the conviction of which I never lose.—ONE conviction in particular remains with me amidst all fluctuations of temper and spirits. I mean my belief of the maxim in my text, that he *who walketh uprightly walketh surely*. There has not been a moment in which I have found it possible to doubt, whether the wisest and best course I can take is to practise virtue and to avoid guilt. Low spirits only give new force to this conviction, and cause it to make a deeper impression. Uncertainty in other instances *creates* certainty here; for the more dark and doubtful our state under God's government is, the more prudent it must be to chuse that course which is the *safest*.

I will

I will only farther defire you to confider on this fubject, with that ferenity of mind a good man may proceed through life. Whatever is true or falfe, he has the confcioufnefs of being on the *fafe* fide; and there is, in all cafes, a particular fatisfaction attending fuch a confcioufnefs. A man who knows himfelf in a fafe way goes on with compofure and boldnefs.—Thus may you go on in a courfe of well-doing. You have none of thofe calamities to fear to which others are liable. If the doctrines of religion are true, you will be completely happy through the Saviour of mankind. But fhould they *not* prove true, you will not be worfe off than others. I have fhewn, on the contrary, that you will ftill be gainers.—Your lofs, in fhort, *can* be *nothing*. Your gain *may* be *infinite*. —Forfake, then, every thing to follow righteoufnefs. Never confent to do a wrong action, or to gratify an unlawful paffion. This will give you a fecurity that is worth more than all the treafures of the earth.
You

You may alſo, on all principles, entertain the *apprehenſion* that the goſpel has given right information concerning the abolition of death, and the happineſs reſerved for the faithful, in the future kingdom of Jeſus Chriſt. That perſon muſt have conſidered the arguments for Chriſtianity very ſuperficially, who does not ſee, that they amount to an evidence, which is at leaſt ſufficient to give a juſt ground for this *apprehenſion*; and, conſequently, for a *hope* the moſt animating and glorious. Let us cheriſh this hope; and endeavour to keep the object of it always in ſight.— The ſlighteſt GLIMPSE of that ETERNAL LIFE which the New Teſtament promiſes, is enough to elevate above this world. The bare *poſſibility* of loſing it, by ſinful practiſes, is enough to annihilate all temptations. Wherefore; *let us be ſtedfaſt and immoveable, always abounding in the work of the Lord, foraſmuch as we know that our labour* MAY *end in a bliſsful eternity*; *but,* happen what will, CANNOT *be in vain.*

SERMON VII.

OF THE HAPPINESS OF A VIRTUOUS COURSE.

PROVERBS iii. 17.

Her ways are ways of pleasantness, and all her paths are peace. She is a tree of life to them that lay hold of her; and happy is every one that receiveth her.

IN my last discourse I represented to you the *security* of a virtuous course. In doing this, I was led to touch upon its tendency to make us most *happy*, as well as most *secure*, under God's government.—I shall now insist more particularly on this subject; and endeavour to give you a distinct account of the principal arguments and facts which prove the happiness of virtue; meaning, on this occasion chiefly, its *present* happiness.

The ways of wisdom (my text says) *are ways of pleasantness; and happy is every one that receiveth her.*—Previously to any examination of the *actual* state of mankind, we may perceive a high probability that this assertion must be true. Virtue is the image of God in the soul, and the noblest thing in the creation; and, therefore, it must be the principal ground of true happiness. It is the rule by which God meant that we should act; and, therefore, must be the way to the bliss for which he intended us. That Being who gave us our sense of moral obligations, must have designed that we should conform to them; and he could not design this, and at the same time design that we should find it most for our advantage *not* to conform to them. This would have been to establish an inconsistency in the frame

frame of nature; and acting in a manner which cannot be supposed of that Supreme power which, in every other part of nature, has discovered higher wisdom than we are able to comprehend.

But waving such reasonings, let us apply ourselves to the consideration of the *actual* state of mankind in this respect. And,

First, Let us consider, that by practising virtue we gratify the highest powers in our natures.—Our highest powers are, undoubtedly, our sense of moral excellence, the principle of reason and reflexion, benevolence' to our fellow-creatures, and the love of the Deity. To practise virtue is to act in conformity to these powers, and to furnish them with their proper gratifications. Our other powers, being inferior to these and of less dignity, the happiness grounded upon them is also of an inferior nature, and of less value. Reason is the *nature* of a reasonable

sonable being; and to assert that his chief happiness consists in deviating from reason, would be the same as to say that his chief happiness consists in violating his *nature*, and contradicting *himself*.

Secondly, In connexion with this we ought to remember, that virtue, in the very idea of it, implies health and order of mind. The human soul is a composition of various affections standing in different relations to one another; and all placed under the direction of conscience, our supreme faculty. When we are truly virtuous, none of these affections are suffered to err either by excess or defect. They are kept in their proper subordinations to one another. The faculty that was made to govern preserves its authority; and a due balance is maintained among our inward powers. To be virtuous, therefore, is to be in our natural and sound state. It is to be freed from all inward tumult, anarchy, and tyranny. It is to enjoy health, and order, and

and vigour, and peace, and liberty; and, therefore, the greatest happiness.—Vice, on the contrary, is slavery, disorder, and sickness. It distorts our inward frame, and unsettles the adjustments of our minds. It unduly raises some of our powers, and depresses others. It dethrones conscience, and subjects it to the despotism of blind and lawless appetites. In short; there is the same difference, in respect of happiness, between a virtuous and a vicious soul, as there is between a *distempered* body and a body that is *well*; or, between a civil state where confusion, faction, and licentiousness reign; and a state where order prevails, and all keep their proper places, and unite in submission to a wise and good legislature.

Again thirdly; It is worth our consideration, that, by practising virtue, we again more of the united pleasures, arising from the gratification of *all* our powers, than we can in any other way. That is, in other words; our moral powers, when prevalent, encroach lefs on the inferior enjoyments of our natures than any of our other powers when *they* are prevalent. In order to explain this, I would defire you to confider, that the courfe moft favourable to happinefs, muft be that which takes from us the leaft that is poffible of any of the gratifications and enjoyments we are capable of. We can take no courfe that will give us an equal and full fhare of all the gratifications of our appetites. If we will gain the ends of fome of our affections, me muft facrifice others. If, for inftance, we will rife to fame and power, we muft give up eafe and pleafure. We muft cringe and truckle, and do violence to fome of our ftrongeft inclinations. In like manner; if we make money our principal purfuit, and would acquire wealth; we muft often contradict our defires of fame and honour. We muft keep down generofity and benevolence, and the love of fenfual indulgences. We muft pinch, and toil, and watch, and eat

eat the bread of carefulness.—An *ambitious* man muſt ſacrifice the gratifications of the *covetous* man. A *covetuous* man, likewiſe, muſt ſacrifice the indulgences of a *man of pleaſure:* And a *man of pleaſure* thoſe of the *ambitious* and *worldly minded.*—Since, then, in *every* courſe of life, there is ſuch an interference between the ſeveral objects of our affections, that courſe in which there is the *leaſt* of it, muſt be likely to make us moſt happy. And it is certain, that there is leſs of it in a virtuous courſe than any other. Virtue brings with it many exquiſite pleaſures of its own (as I ſhall preſently obſerve more particularly) and, at the ſame time, does not neceſſarily encroach on other ſources of pleaſure. It is the very beſt means of obtaining the ends of moſt of our *lower* powers and affections. It is, for inſtance, the beſt means of gaining honour and diſtinction among our fellow-creatures; for the virtuous man is always the man who is moſt honoured and loved.

It

It is, likewise, one of the best means of becoming prosperous in our affairs, and gaining a competent share of worldly blessings; for, agreeably to a maxim which we hear often repeated, "honesty is the best policy." A virtuous man is the man who is most industrious, and likely to be most encouraged and trusted in every trade and profession.—In short; it is a part of virtue to make use chearfully of all the materials of happiness with which Divine bounty has supplied us. There is no lawful and natural pleasure of which it does not leave us in possession. It is favourable to every innocent pursuit, and an excellent friend to every just and laudable undertaking.

These observations remove entirely the objection to the happiness of virtue, taken from its requiring labour and circumspection, and obliging us to restrain our passions, and to practise self-denial. It is, indeed, true, that virtue requires this: But you should recollect, that it is by no means

means peculiar to virtue. I have, on the contrary, been shewing that it is less applicable to virtue than to any other object of pursuit.—What labour and self-denial do men often practise in pursuing fame, or honour, or money? What a sacrifice does the man of pleasure make of his health and fortune; and to what fatigues does he often put himself?—It is, therefore, the utmost injustice to virtue to imagine that the restraint of inclination, and the practise of self-denial, are peculiar to it. These are common to virtue and vice, and necessary whatever course we take.—It would be very unreasonable to mention as an objection here, that virtue may oblige us to sacrifice to it even our lives. For this is what happens perpetually in vicious courses. Thousands are every day dying martyrs to ambition, to lust, to covetousness, and intemperance. But seldom does it happen, that virtue puts us to any such trial. On the contrary; its

general

general effect is to preserve and lengthen life.

It ought to be particularly observed on this occasion, that, in comparing the influence of different courses on our happiness, we should consider the influence they have on our moral and intellectual powers, as well as our other powers. Conscience is one important part of our natures. To leave it out, therefore, in forming a scheme of enjoyment, or in determining what course will bring us most happiness, would be preposterous and wild. That a course of conduct obliges us to run counter to our sense of moral good and evil, and to give up the satisfactions founded on this sense, ought to be allowed its just weight in judging of the happiness of an agent; and to be considered as a circumstance diminishing his pleasures, in the same manner as if he ran counter to any of his other powers, or gave up any other gratifications.—Now, every species of vice interferes directly
with

with our sense of moral good and evil. It gratifies one part of our natures at the expence of onr judgment and reason; and this is as much an argument proving its hurtfulness, as if it opposed our desires of ease, or honour, or any of our other particular affections. There is, therefore, on this account, a severe and cruel self-denial in vice. At the same time that it encroaches on many of the lower springs of action, it puts a force upon the highest. It obliges us to *deny* our consciences; and, these being most properly *ourselves*, it obliges us to practise a more proper and unnatural self-denial than any denial of passion and appetite.

But to say no more on this head. What I have meant chiefly to inculcate is, that the course most conducive to happiness must be that which is most agreeable to our *whole* natures; and that, this being evidently true of a virtuous course, it follows that it is our greatest happiness.

Hitherto,

Hitherto, you have seen, that I have argued for the happiness of virtue from the considerations, " that it affords our " highest powers their proper gratificati-" ons; that it implies health, and liberty, " and order of mind; and that it is more " agreeable than any other end we can " pursue, to all the parts of our natures " taken as making together one system." There is a great deal more to be said, to which I must request your attention; for

Fourthly, It deserves your consideration, that much of the pleasure of vice itself depends on some species or other of virtue combined with it. All the joys we derive from friendship, from family connexions and affinities, from the love and confidence of our fellow-creatures, and from the intercourse of good offices, are properly *virtuous* joys: And there is no course of life which, were it deprived of these joys, would not be completely miserable. The enjoyments, therefore, of vicious

ous men are owing to the remains of virtuous qualities in them.—There is no man so vicious as to have nothing good left in his character; and could we conceive any such man; or meet with a person who was quite void of benevolence, temperance, good-humour, sociableness, and honour; we should detest him as an odious monster, and find that he was incapable of all happiness. Wickedness, when considered by itself and in its naked form, without any connexion with lovely qualities, is nothing but shame, and pain, and distress. If the *debauchee* enjoys any thing like happiness, it is because he joins to his debauchery something laudable; and his tender and social feelings are not extirpated. In like manner; if a *covetous* man has any thing besides perplexity and gloominess in his heart, it is because there are some virtues which he practises, or because he disguises his covetousness under the forms of the virtues of prudence and frugality.
—This

—This then being the cafe; since even the pleasure that vice enjoys is thus founded upon and derived from virtuous qualities, how plain is it that these constitute our chief good; and that the more of them we possess, so much the more must we possess of the sources of pleasure?—The virtuous man is the most generous man, the most friendly, the most good-natured, the most patient and contented. He has most of the satisfactions resulting from sympathy, and humanity, and natural affection; and so certain is it, that such a person must be the happiest, that the wicked themselves, if in any respect happy, can be so only as far as they either *are* the same that he is, or *think* themselves the same.

Fifthly, I have already observed, that virtues leaves us in possession of all the common enjoyments of life. It is necessary now to add, that it goes much beyond

yond this.—It not only leaves us in pofſeſſion of all innocent and natural pleaſures; but improves and refines them. It not only interferes *leſs* with the gratification of our different powers than vice does; but renders the gratification of many of them *more* the cauſe of pleaſure. This effect it produces by reſtraining us to regularity and moderation in the gratification of our deſires. Virtue forbids only the wild and extravagant gratification of our deſires: That is; it forbids only ſuch a gratification of them as goes beyond the bounds of nature, and lays the foundation of pain and miſery. As far as they were deſigned by our Maker to yield pleaſure, we are at liberty to indulge them; and farther we cannot go without loſing pleaſure.—It is a truth generally acknowledged, that the regular and moderate gratification of appetite is more agreeable than any forced and exorbitant gratification of it. Exceſs in every way is painful and pernicious. We can never

never contradict nature without suffering, and bringing upon ourselves inconveniences.—Is there any man to whom food and sleep are so pleasant as to the temperate man? Are the mad and polluted joys of the fornicator and adulterer equal to the pure and chaste joys of the married state? Do pampered and loaded appetites afford as much delight as appetites kept under discipline, and never palled by riot and licentiousness? Is the vile glutton, the loathsome drunkard, or the rotten debauchee, as happy as the sober and virtuous man who has a healthful body, a serene mind, and general credit?

Thus is virue a friend even to appetite. But this is not the observation I intended to insist on. What I meant here principally to recommend to your attention was, that virtue improves all the blessings of life, by putting us into a particular disposition for receiving pleasure from them. It removes those internal evils which pollute and impair the springs of enjoyment within

within us. It renders the mind easy and satisfied within itself, and therefore more susceptible of delight, and more open to all agreeable impressions.—It is a common observation, that the degree of pleasure which we receive from any objects depends on the disposition we are in to receive pleasure. Nothing is sweet to a depraved taste; nothing beautiful to a distempered eye. This observation holds with particular force in the present case. Vice destroys the relish of sensible pleasures. It takes off (I may say) from the fruit its flavour, and from the rose its hue. It tarnishes the beauty of nature, and communicates a bitter tincture to every enjoyment.—Virtue, on the contrary, sweetens every blessing, and throws new lustre on the face of nature. It chases away gloominess and peevishness; and, by strengthening the kind affections and introducing into the soul good humour and tranquillity, makes every pleasing scene and occurrence more pleasing.

Again

Again sixthly; Let us consider how many *peculiar* joys virtue has which nothing else can give. It is not possible to enumerate all these. We may, on this occasion, recollect first those joys which necessarily spring from the worthy and generous affections. The love of the Deity, benevolence, meekness, and gratitude, are by their nature attended with pleasure. They put the mind into a serene and chearful frame, and introduce into it some of the most delightful sensations. Virtue consists in the exercise and cultivation of these principles. They form the temper and constitute the character of a virtuous man; and, therefore, he must enjoy pleasures to which men of a contrary character are strangers.—It is not conceivable, that a person in whom the mild and generous affections thrive, should not be in a more happy state than one who counteracts and suppresses them; and who, instead of feeling the joy which springs up in a heart where the heavenly graces

graces and virtues reside, is torn and distracted by anger, malice, and envy.

But farther; Peace of conscience is another blessing peculiar to virtue. It reconciles us to ourselves as well as to all the world. As nothing can be so horrid as to be at variance with one's self, so nothing can be so delightful as to be at peace with one's self. If we are unhappy within our own breasts, it signifies little what external advantages we enjoy. If we want *our own* approbation, it is of little consequence how much *others* applaud us. Virtue secures to us our own approbation. It reduces to harmony, under the dominion of conscience, all our jarring powers. It makes our reflexions agreeable to us; and the mind a fund of comfort to itself.

Again; A sense of God's favour is another source of pleasure which is peculiar to virtue. The Divine government is an object of terror to a wicked man. He cannot think of it without trouble. But a vira virtuous man derives his chief confolations from hence. He is confcious of acting in concert with the Deity, of obeying his laws, and of imitating his perfections. He, therefore, exults in the affurance of having him on his fide, and of being under his Almighty protection. He knows that the Sovereign of the univerfe loves him, and is his unalterable friend.

Once more. A virtuous man poffeffes the hope of a future reward. Every one knows how mighty the power of hope is to invigorate and chear the mind. There is no fuch hope as that of the virtuous man. He hopes for a perfect government in the heavens; and this comforts him amidft all the diforders of earthly governments. He hopes for a refurrection from death to the bleffed immortality. He expects foon to take poffeffion of a treafure in the heavens that faileth not; to receive an incorruptible inheritance; to exchange ignorance and doubt for knowledge; and to to be fixed in that world where he shall join superior beings, and be always growing more wise, and good, and great, and happy, till some time or other he shall rise to honours and powers which are no more possible to be now conceived by him, than the powers of an angel can be conceived by a child in the womb.—This is indeed an unbounded and ravishing hope. If Christianity is true, we have abundant reason for it. Christ came into the world to raise us to it; and the most distant glimmering of it is enough to eclipse all the glory of this world.

Such are the singular blessings of the virtuous man.

Let us, in the next place, take into consideration some peculiar qualities of the happiness now described. This will complete our view of this subject, and render it unnecessary to add any thing to convince an attentive person of the truth I am insisting upon. Virtue has a great deal

deal of *peculiar* happiness; and that happiness has many excellent qualities which belong to no other happiness. — It is, for instance, more *permanent* than any other happiness. The pleasures of the vicious are *transient*; but virtue is a spring of *constant* pleasure and satisfaction. The pleasures which attend the gratification of our appetites soon pall. They are gone for ever after the moment of gratification; and, when carried to excess, they turn to pain and disgust. But nothing like this can be said of the pleasures of virtue. These never cloy or satiate. They can never be carried to excess. They are always new and fresh. They may be repeated as often as we please without losing their relish. They are such as will not only *bear* repetition and reflexion, but are *improved* by them. They will go with us to all places; and attend us through every changing scene of life. No inclosures of stone or iron, no intervention of seas and kingdoms can

keep

keep them from us. They delight alike at home and abroad; by day and by night; in the city and in the defart.—The aid of wine and of company is not neceffary to enable us to enjoy them. They are, in truth, enjoyed in the greateft perfection when the mind, collecting itfelf within itfelf, and withdrawing itfelf from all worldly objects, fixes its attention only on its own ftate and profpects.

It follows from thefe obfervations, that the happinefs of virtue is a more *independent* happinefs than any other. It is, if I may fo fpeak, more *one* with the foul; and, therefore, lefs fubject to the operations of external caufes. The pleafure arifing from the confcioufnefs of having done a worthy action, of having relieved a diftreft family, or fubdued our anger, our envy, or our impatience; this is a pleafure which enters into the very fubftance of the foul, and cannot be torn from it without tearing it from itfelf, and deftroying its exiftence.—All other pleafures sures are precarious in the highest degree. We have but little power over them; and they may be taken from us the next moment in spite of our strongest efforts to retain them. But the joy connected with right action, with a self-approving heart, and the hope of a glorious eternity, no accidents can take away. These are *inward* blessings which are not liable to be affected by *outward* causes; and which produce a happiness that is immutable, and not possible to be lost except with our own consent.

There is nothing that the ancient philosophers have taken so much pains to inculcate, as the importance of placing our happiness only in things within our power. If we place it in fame, or money, or any external good, it will have a most deceitful foundation, and we shall be liable to perpetual disappointment: Whereas, if we place it in the exercise of virtuous affections, in traquillity of mind, in regular passions, in doing God's will, and the hope

hope of his favour; we shall have it always at our command. We shall never be liable to disappointments. We shall find true rest to our souls; and be in a situation like to that of a person lifted to the upper regions of the atmosphere, who hears thunder roll, and sees lightenings flash and the clouds spread below him, while he enjoys serenity and sunshine.

I must add, that the happiness of virtue is a *pure* and *refined* happiness. It is seated in the mind. Other happiness has its seat in the body.—It is the happiness of angels. Other happiness is the happiness of brutes.—It must, therefore, be also the most solid, the most substantial and exalted happiness. I observe this, because I belive the generality of men are disposed to look upon no happiness as solid, which is purely spiritual. What I have just said affords a demonstration of the contrary. The most exalted happiness must be that of superior being.

beings, of angels, and of the Deity. But this is a happiness that is spiritual, and which has no connexion with the gratifications of sense. The happiness of the virtuous, therefore, being of the same kind, it must be the most real and substantial.

To say no more on this head. Let me desire you to consider, that the happiness of the virtuous man continues with him even in affliction. This is one of the most distinguishing properties of this happiness. Virtue, as it increases the relish of prosperity, blunts likewise the edge of adversity. It is, indeed, in adversity, that the power of virtue to make us happy appears to the greatest advantage. It kindles a light in the soul in the darkest seasons; and very often produces then the highest bliss when animal nature is at the lowest, and other joys have deserted us.—There is, in this respect, a most striking difference between the condition of the virtuous and vicious man.

In

In adverſity the vicious man becomes completely wretched. He has no comfortable reflexions to ſupport him; no protecting Deity to truſt in; no proſpect of future bleſſings to encourage him. Wherever he turns his eyes all is confuſion and diſtreſs. Reaſon and conſcience have him to themſelves, and inflict the ſharpeſt ſufferings.—But the virtuous man, in adverſity, may rejoice and exult. Whatever he now ſuffers, he may be aſſured that all will end happily. When fleſh and heart ſink under him, faith and hope and charity unite their influence to ſuſtain him. A heavenly voice whiſpers peace to him when all about him ſpeaks terror; and the conſolations of God delight his ſoul when the ſprings of worldly comfort are dried up.—Particularly; in the ſolemn hour of death he has reaſon to be compoſed and chearful. That is the hour which ſeals the vicious man under ruin; but it confirms and perfects the happineſs of the virtuous man, and ſets

him

him free for ever from pain and danger. He can, therefore, look forward to it without disturbance, and meet it joyfully.—Religious and virtuous principles, if they have their due efficacy, will enable us to die with dignity and triumph. They will change the aspect of the king of terrors into that of a friend and deliverer, and cause us to desire and welcome his stroke.

Thus have I shewn you that religious virtue is our chief good. And we may now, with full conviction, take up the words of my text, and say with *Solomon*, *That her ways are ways of pleasantness, and that all her paths are peace; that she is a tree of life to them that lay hold of her; and that happy is every one that receiveth her.*

I will only farther desire your attention to the following inferences.

First. How wrong is it to conceive of religious virtue as an enemy to pleasure? This is doing it the greatest injustice. It is, is, without all doubt, the very best friend to true pleasure.—Were we indeed to judge of it from the stiffness and severity of some who pretend to it, we might be forced to entertain a different opinion of it. But such persons do not shew it us in its true form. They mistake its nature, and are strangers to its genuine spirit.— One part of the duty it requires of us, is to accept thankfully every innocent gratification of life, and to *rejoice ever more*. Instead of driving us, with the wretched votaries of superstition, into desarts and cloisters, and making us morose and gloomy; it calls us out into society, and disposes us to constant alacrity and chearfulness.

Secondly. What strong evidence have we for the moral government of the Deity? You have seen that he has so constituted nature that virtue is, by its necessary tendency, our greatest bliss. He is, therefore, on the side of virtue. By establishing the connexion I have been representing

senting between it and happiness, he has declared himself its friend in a manner the most decisive. What we see takes place of this connexion in the present life is the beginning of a moral government; and it should lead us to expect a future life, where what is now begun will be compleated—where every present irregularity will be set right—virtue receive its *full* reward, and vice its *full* punishment.

Lastly. What reasons have we for seeking virtue above all things? You have heard how happy it will make us. Let us then pray for it earnestly; and despise every thing that can come in competition with it. If we *have* this, we can *want* nothing that is desirable. If we *want* this, we can *have* nothing that will do us any substantial service.—Go then all ye careless and irreligious men. Take to yourselves your money, your honours, and polluted pleasures. I would desire VIRTUE only. There is nothing else worth an eager wish. Here would I center

center all my cares and labours. May God grant me this, and deny me what else he pleases. This is his choicest blessing; his best and richest gift. This is that tree of life whose leaf never withers, and whose fruit will revive us in every hour of dejection, cure all our maladies, and prolong our existence to endless ages; for, as St. Paul speaks, if *we have our fruit unto holiness, our end will be* EVERLASTING LIFE.

SERMON VIII.

OF THE GOODNESS OF GOD.

PSALMS xxxiv. 8.

O taste and see that the Lord is good. Blessed is the man that trusteth in him.

THE titles GREATEST and BEST, have in all ages been applied to the Deity. We are led to this by the unavoidable sentiments and perceptions of our minds. The first and uncreated being must be the GREATEST; and the GREATEST must likewise be the BEST; for true greatness includes in it goodness. Almighty power, universal dominion,

dominion, and infinite knowledge confidered by themfelves, can excite no other emotions than awe and terror. They have in them none of that dignity which engages veneration, except they are accompanied with benevolence. This is the crown of all the attributes of the Deity. It is this finifhes his character; and nothing can be of more importance to us than a thorough conviction of it, and juft fentiments concerning it. If we either do not believe it, or entertain unworthy apprehenfions of it as partial or capricious; fome of the principal comforts of our exiftence muft be loft; and our religious fervices muft become an abject and illiberal drudgery and fuperftition. I cannot, therefore, be better employed than in endeavouring to explain and prove to you God's goodnefs; and this I propofe to make my bufinefs in the prefent difcourfe; after which, I fhall, in a future difcourfe, infift particularly on the practical improvement of it.

This

This is a subject of a very extensive nature; and, were I to enter into a particular and full discussion of it, I should take up a great deal of your time. But I shall endeavour to avoid prolixity, and aim only at making such observations as appear to me most useful and important, without entering far into abstruse enquiries.

GOODNESS, when applied to the Deity, may be considered in two views. It may signify either the *principle* itself of goodness; that is, that benevolence of disposition which leads to the communication of happiness; or, it may signify, the *exercise* of this principle in the *actual* communication of happiness. We use, in common language, the word goodness sometimes in the former of these senses, and sometimes in the latter; and it is of some importance that we take care to distinguish them. Much may be said of the *principle* of goodness in the Deity which cannot, without great impropriety, be

applied

applied to the *exercise* of it in the creation and government of the world.—In particular, it may be justly said of God's goodness, in the former sense, that it is *necessary*. His nature is benevolence; and a disposition to communicate happiness is inseparable from it. There is as much a physical impossibility of his wanting this disposition as there is of his wanting power or knowledge, or even existence.—But the same cannot be said of his goodness in the latter sense. Though the disposition to communicate happiness is necessary in him, yet the *exercise* of it (that is, every act proceeding from this disposition) is perfectly free. And this is one of the chief observations to which I would desire you to attend on this subject. You should always think of God's goodness as an unconstrained and free goodness. All its effects proceed, not from irresistible necessity, but from voluntary choice. He has it in his power not to confer on his creatures the blessings they enjoy: Nor is

it

it the least objection to this, that the *principle* of goodness within him is, as I have said, necessary. We experience in ourselves that the principles or motives of action within us are necessary, though our actions themselves are free. Thus, self-love is essential to us. We can no more divest ourselves of it than we can of our beings. But the actions derived from it are free; and we have a power not to perform them.—In like manner; the preference of virtue is absolutely necessary; but, at the same time, we find that we can, if we please, determine not to follow this preference. In other words; dispositions and views, arising from unavoidable principles in beings, are only the motives and occasions of their determinations. They only shew, how an action is to be accounted for; not its efficient cause. This must always be the self-determination of the agent.—It has, I know, been objected to this, that it tends to destroy the immutability of

God's moral perfections. But no objection can be less reasonable. In lower instances, we cannot wish for any greater certainty than that which depends only on the voluntary determinations of agents in particular circumstances. It would, indeed, be intolerably absurd to imagine that the Deity is not good *immutably*, because he is so *freely*; or to conclude, that he will make his creatures miserable, because it is in his power to do it. Nothing can be more certain than that perfect righteousness will never act unrighteously, or perfect goodness cruelly: And this is not the less a certainty, because it is founded on choice, and not on any physical necessity. Were this the foundation of certainty in this case; or, were the Deity good in all his actions by the same necessity by which he exists, we could not perceive any *moral* excellence in his goodness; and it would be as impossible to think it an object of grati-

gratitude, as to think so of his eternity and immensity.

But I have dwelt, perhaps, too long on this observation. I will, therefore, hasten to desire you to remember, in connexion with it, that God's goodness is not to be considered as a propensity within him of which no account is to be given from REASON. This is a notion which some have entertained of it. But nothing can detract more from its honour. According to this opinion, public happiness and public misery are the same to intellectual discernment. A reasonable being *as such* is incapable of preferring the one to the other; and, therefore, necessarily void of benevolence, except as the effect of some bias or affection within him, prior in the order of our ideas to reason, and independent of it. It is not wisdom, then, or intelligence, that makes the Deity benevolent; for wisdom, according to this account, can never give rise to a preference of any ends, but is employed
only

only in directing to the best means of attaining an end.—It is surprising that such a sentiment should have found a place in the minds of able and ingenious men. Indeed, I can scarcely think, that we are certain of any thing, if it be not true that goodness, considered as a principle of action, is a disposition that arises necessarily in an *intelligent* nature [a]. And I wish you to remember, in opposition to this opinion, that God's goodness is a *reasonable* goodness; a principle founded in reason, derived from reason, and under the direction of reason in all its operations. In mankind there are two springs of our affections—instinctive determination and reason.—But we must take care to remove the former entirely from the Deity

[a] A particular discussion of this question, together with a more full account of the proof here insisted on, of God's goodness taken from its connexion with his intelligence, may be found in my Treatise on Morals, chap. i. iii. & x.

Deity in our conceptions of him. He can poffefs nothing analogous to any of the inftinctive principles and inclinations which have been given us. He is pure and perfect reafon; and perfect reafon is in him the true fpring of every moral principle which we afcribe to him; and, particularly, of his infinite goodnefs. He purfues general happinefs as his end, becaufe it is in itfelf a right end and worthy of his choice.

But this leads me to mention to you the chief argument which proves the goodnefs of God. It is included in his intelligence. Benevolence is an affection which arifes as necefsarily in an *intelligent* nature, as felf-love does in a *fenfitive* nature. Moral diftinctions are founded in truth; and every being who perceives truth muft perceive them. The Deity, therefore, who perceives all truth, muft perceive them in all their extent and obligation, and be more under their influence than any other being.—The chief of of all moral diſtinctions is this—" that " it is *right* to communicate happineſs, " and *wrong* to produce miſery."—This diſtinction, therefore, in particular, God as intelligent muſt perceive; and the perception of it is the very ſame with the approbation of beneficence, and the diſ-approbation of its contrary.—I cannot think of a ſtronger argument.—It ſhews us, that the principle of benevolence in the Deity is implied in his perception of truth; and that it is juſt as certain that he is good, as it is that we ſay right when we ſay, that " happineſs is better than " miſery."

It may, I know, be enquired here, whether (though it thus appears that God is benevolent) there may not be ſome oppoſite principles in his nature (like thoſe in ourſelves) which may have a tendency to lead him aſtray from benevolence?— In anſwer to this, it ſhould be remembered, that the argument I have mentioned not only proves that he is benevolent,

lent, but that he is so, as much more perfectly than any other being as his intelligence is more perfect; or, that he is as much more under the influence of benevolence as he knows truth and right better. In reality; truth and right and goodness are *himself*; and the Scriptures assert what is more literally just than is commonly apprehended, when it tells us, that "God is love."—The natures of happiness and misery are' such, that a preference of one of them to the other must arise in every mind in proportion to the degree in which they are known. The natures of things have their foundation in the nature of the Deity. In him, therefore, every preference or affection that has its foundation in the natures of things must take place in its completest and highest degree; and, more particularly, the principle of rectitude must in him for this reason be sovereign and perfect, and not uncertain, feeble, and precarious as in inferior beings.—In a word; since benevolence

volence is a part of the idea of intelligence, it follows, with the plainest evidence, that the *Supreme* intelligence must be original and *supreme* benevolence; or such a benevolence as nothing can turn aside, or deceive, or counteract.

The suspicion, therefore, that there may be principles in the Deity which interfere with goodness and incline him to malevolence, is unreasonable and groundless. His nature is perfect and eternal reason; and in such a nature there can be no tendencies which are not derived from reason; much less, any that clash with reason. He is what he is necessarily: But the same necessity cannot, without a contradiction, be supposed to be the ground of the approbation of beneficence, and, at the same time, of biasses inconsistent with it.

The causes that lead us astray from goodness are partial views, the impulses of passion, defects of power, and private interest. But he cannot be
in-

influenced by any of these causes of deviation. He is omniscient; and, therefore, subject to no partial views. He is self-existent; and, therefore, infinitely removed from the possibility of all instinctive principles. He is Almighty; and, therefore, incapable of being disappointed or controuled. He is independent and self sufficient; and, therefore, can have no interest separate from that of the beings he has created.

The argument I have now insisted on is, I believe, that to which men have always chiefly owed their belief of the goodness of the Deity. What most naturally leads us to apply to him this attribute, seems to be our apprehension of excellence in it; or the discernment we have that it is *right* to communicate happiness, and *wrong* to give pain.—But I should not be excusable, did I not turn your thoughts to another argument of the utmost

utmoſt conſequence. I mean, that taken from the effects of goodneſs which we ſee in the creation.

Theſe two arguments united are, I think, when duly attended to, ſufficient to give us complete ſatisfaction.

Our reaſonings on this point, from the natures of things, are confirmed by obſervation and experience. When we conſult our own ideas (without attending to what takes place without us) we perceive a neceſſary union between infinite power, wiſdom, and goodneſs. Where there is infinite power, there muſt be infinite knowledge; and, ſince moral diſtinctions are (as I have ſaid) founded in truth, where there is infinite knowledge, there muſt be infinite goodneſs.—There can be nothing ſo encouraging and joyous as the reflexion on this truth. But the joy it gives is greatly increaſed by the additional reflexion, that there is the ſame union of theſe attributes in the conſtitution of the world, that we ſee in the natures of things

and

and find in our own ideas. The ftate of the creation actually correfponds to what, in this inftance, reafon, independently of experience, teaches us to believe of the firft caufe. Wherever we fee power and fkill difplayed, we alfo fee goodnefs difplayed. Wherever we fee defign, we fee it to be not only *wife* defign, but *kind* defign. The primary tendency of all the laws of nature with which we are acquainted is to happinefs and enjoyment. The fruits of benevolence are fcattered through the world; and, therefore, the Maker muft be benevolent. An univerfe fo harmonious and fair, fo orderly and beautiful, and fo peopled with numberlefs varieties of living beings all rejoicing in exiftence, all liberally provided for, and enjoying bleffings fuitable to their natures and fituations.—Such an univerfe could never proceed from an evil or felfifh or malicious being.—Every new object we meet with, every new difcovery we make, and every ftep we advance in the knowledge of God's works, affords us new reasons for admiring the glory of his perfections, and for adoring and praising him.

But I am sensible it will be objected here.—Is there not evil in the world as well as good? And how can this be accounted for, if the Author of the world is perfectly good? Would he not, had this been true, have excluded from the creation every groan and pang?—These are enquiries which offer themselves naturally to every person in thinking on this subject. Were I to attempt making as particular a reply to them as their importance deserves, I should go much beyond the limits which I have prescribed to myself. I am in hopes, however, that you will think the following brief observations sufficient.

First. It should be remembered, that the evil which there is in the world is overbalanced by good. We should, in this case, judge of the intention of the Deity by by what *prevails* in his works; and this, without doubt, is happinefs. Though we often fee many individuals fuffering pain, and fometimes groaning under heavy calamities, yet this is by no means the *general* ſtate of the world. All the tribes of animals about us were plainly made for happinefs; and their natural and ordinary ſtate is a ſtate of health and fome degree of enjoyment. Pain and diſtrefs are out of the common courfe of nature; and this caufes them to be over-rated and magnified whenever they happen. One bad fit of illnefs is remembered and talked of during life, though compenfated fo far as to be almoſt annihilated, by many years of health and eafe and comfort.—Indeed, I believe the excefs of enjoyment above abfolute mifery, in the exiſtence of all living creatures, is much greater than we are willing to allow; and the latter, could we compare it fairly with the former and judge of it properly, would appear no more to us than the fhades are in a fine picture,

picture, or the difcords in a grand concert.

But fecondly. It fhould be confidered that a great part of the evil in the world appears plainly to be the neceffary means of good, and to be intended for this purpofe.—The former obfervation would be alone fufficient to vindicate God's goodnefs in the permiffion of evil; for it is extremely unreafonable to imagine, that every being ought, during its whole exiftence, to be exempted from every degree of pain. What goodnefs requires is the production of happinefs; and this is *equally* produced whether the happinefs of a being is fo much enjoyment unmixed with pain, or the fame degree of enjoyment confifting of a clear excefs of pleafure above pain. But we need not reft in this obfervation. The pains mixed with the enjoyments of beings are neceffary to thofe enjoyments. They appear to be defigned, not for their own fakes, but always for the fake of fome good connected with

with them, or of some particular benefit to the beings who suffer them.—The pains of hunger, for instance, are necessary to put us upon taking food. The pains, occasioned by a wound or by diseases, are necessary to engage us to take proper care of our bodies; and, without such pains, we should so far neglect ourselves, as to be in danger of perishing by every malady that seized us, and by every accident we met with. In like manner; the pains of self-reproach and remorse are necessary to restrain us from wickedness, and to keep us in the path of virtue and duty.—In these, and numberless other instances, our pains are salutary and kindly intended. They are remedies for evil, and preservatives from danger and misery; and, therefore, instead of furnishing an argument against God's goodness, they are as much proofs of it as any of our pleasures.

In connexion with this I must mention to you, that many of the evils we complain of are effects of regulations and establishments in the universe which are necessary to produce the greatest happiness.—It is absolutely necessary, that the affairs of the universe should be governed by general laws, operating uniformly and invariably in given circumstances. Were not this the constitution of nature, there would be no such thing as a regular course of nature; no one would know what to expect from any thing he did; and there could be no prudence, no foresight, no room for the exercise of any of the active powers of beings. But, at the same time, it is obvious, that the consequence of such a constitution must be, in some instances, pains and sufferings. The consequence, for instance, of the universal operation of the law of gravitation must be sometimes broken limbs and untimely deaths: But he that should, for this reason, allow himself to wish there were no such law; or that it were suspended whenever it might do any harm; would wish to have the whole frame of nature unhinged, and the

the general happiness destroyed, only for the sake of preventing a few bad accidents. —To the same purpose, it may be observed, that the ends of goodness require that there should be in the universe creatures of all orders; and that there should be a dependence of their states on one another. For, without this, there would be no sphere of agency for beings; no room for the exercise of benevolence by doing good to our fellow-creatures; nor, consequently, any possibility of the practice of virtue in that instance of it which brings us nearest to the perfection of the Deity. A variety, therefore, of orders of beings; a dependence of them on one another; and, in general, imperfections and subordinations among them, and a precariousness of state, are necessary to render that happiness possible which consists in the exercise of the rational and moral powers of beings. But it is obvious, that from hence must arise a liableness to calamities; and, in many circumstances,

stances, the diſtreſs of *individuals*, or sometimes, perhaps, of a *whole species*. —In ſhort. Exclude from the world that liberty which we often ſee ſo dreadfully abuſed: Exclude from it all wants and ſubordinations and dangers and loſſes: Set all beings on a level, and emancipate them entirely from the influence of one another's agency; and you will leave no creature any thing to do. You will lay the whole rational creation aſleep, and exclude from it all that happineſs which is moſt worth producing.

Theſe obſervations are, in my opinion, a ſatisfactory anſwer to the objection I am conſidering. It appears that the evil we ſee is inconſiderable compared with the good; and that it may be the neceſſary conſequence of a conſtitution formed, in the beſt manner, to produce the greateſt happineſs. Notwithſtanding all the abatements to be made on account of the uneaſineſſes and troubles in the world, a juſt eſtimate of its ſtate will convince us, that it it is an effect of inconceivable goodnefs. In order to make it anfwer to the notion of malevolence in its author, it is, in truth, neceffary to reverfe it in almoft every inftance.—I wifh I could here reprefent to you properly, what you might have expected would have been the ftate of the world, had mifery been the ultimate intention of the Deity.

EVIL would, in this cafe, have appeared to be the aim of nature in all its appointments; and GOOD, we fhould have found (as we do *evil* now) to be always the confequence of either fome regulation for producing general mifery, or of fome unnatural violence and perverfion.—All defign in the frame of nature we fhould have feen to be cruel defign; and all that wifdom of God in his works which we now admire and adore, we fhould have dreaded and curfed as a contrivance to extend diftrefs, and to render pain more pungent and permanent.—The *ordinary* ftate of every being we fhould have found
to

to be (not a state of ease and enjoyment) but of trouble, dejection, and anguish. The lower animals, and all inanimate nature, instead of being made to minister to our delight and accommodation, would have been made to annoy and harrass us. The bee would have been without her honey, and the rose without its fragrance. The fields would have wanted their chearful green and gay flowers. The fire would have scorched without warming us. The light of day would have dazzled without chearing us. Every breath of air would have cut us like the point of a sword. The appetites and senses would have been the instruments of torture, and never of pleasure to us, except when turned out of their common course by incidental causes. Every touch would have felt like the rubbing of a wound. Every taste would have been a bitter; and every sound a scream. Our imaginations would have presented nothing but frightful spectres to us. Our thoughts would have

have been the feat of a deep and conftant melancholy; and our reafon would have ferved only to fhew us our wretchednefs. —What we now call *gratification* would have been nothing but a *relaxation* of torment; and we fhould have been driven to the offices neceffary for felf-preferva- tion, by an increafe of fufferings occafioned by neglecting them. Or if, at any time, any feelings of delight were granted us; they would have been (as the paroxifms of pain are at prefent) tranfient and rare, and intended only to fet a keener edge on mifery by giving a tafte of its contrary.— In the prefent ftate of the world our pains, when they become extreme, foon make an end of either themfelves or us: But, in the ftate of things I am imagining, there would have been no fuch merciful appointment; for our bodies, probably, would have been fo made as to be capable of bearing the fevereft pains; and, at the fame time, we might have been deterred

from

from self-violence by knowing, that the consequence of hastening death would be getting sooner into a state of misery still more dreadful, and which should NEVER come to an end.

But it is high time to stop. I know you must hear with horror this representation. Such, however, be assured, and infinitely worse than I can paint, would have been the condition of the world had it been made for misery. The real state of it is, I have shewn, totally different; and from hence it is impossible not to conclude that the Maker of it is benevolent. —We may then rejoice in our existence. We may look up to heaven with triumph. Verily, God is good. This is the dictate of reason. This is the voice of all nature.

I have much more to say on this subject; and I should now go on to make some farther observations in order to assist you in forming just ideas of God's goodness. But

But thefe obfervations, together with a general recital of the effects of God's goodnefs and the practical improvement of it, fhall be referved for another difcourfe.

SERMON IX.

OF THE GOODNESS OF GOD.

PSALMS xxxiv. 8.

O taste and see that the Lord is good. Blessed is the man that trusteth in him.

IN a former discourse from these words, I endeavoured to explain and prove to you the goodness of God. I then insisted, among other arguments, on the traces of goodness, as well as of wisdom, which we see in the works of God. Happiness, I observed, prevails in nature; and all that we know of its constitution and laws shews, that the power which gave birth to it, and which prefides in it, is benevolent.

There is one objection to this argument which I will juſt take notice of, before I proceed to what I principally intend at this time.—It may occur to ſome " that, ſince what we ſee of nature
" is comparatively nothing, it cannot
" afford ſufficient ground for any certain
" concluſion. A malevolent being may
" ſometimes be the cauſe of happineſs, as
" a benevolent being may of ſufferings.
" A ſingle act cannot be enough to give
" a proof of the character of an agent,
" otherwiſe totally unknown to us. From
" what takes place in a *point* and a *mo-*
" *ment*, no judgment can be formed of
" what takes place *univerſally* and *eter-*
" *nally.*"

In anſwer to this objection, I would deſire you to conſider,

Firſt, That, in all caſes, it is moſt reaſonable to judge of what we do *not* know by what we *do* know. We are ſure, fure, that happiness prevails in all that we see of nature; and however little that is, it affords a fair presumption that happiness prevails likewise in the rest of nature.

But secondly, This evidence from fact is confirmed by arguments, taken from the reasons of things and the nature of the first cause, as represented in my former discourse: And, however unsatisfactory this evidence might otherwise have been, it amounts, when taken in this connexion, to one of the strongest proofs. But

Thirdly, The truth is, that this evidence, even when taken by itself, is in a high degree satisfactory, and that the objection I have stated has no tendency to lessen its weight.—The following observation will, I think, shew this.—Whatever the character of the Deity may be, his works must, *upon the whole,* correspond to it. Particular exceptions to this correspondence may possibly take place at particular times in particular districts; but they must, without doubt, be singular and extraordinary. If misery, therefore, is the end of the Deity, there must have been the greatest chance against our being cast into that part of the creation in which misery is *not* prevalent. And this chance is the same whether the creation be more or less extensive.—For this reason, I cannot help reckoning the improbability almost infinite, of our happening to have been brought into existence in that period of duration and district of the universe in which goodness is displayed, if, indeed, goodness is *not* the character of the Deity.—This confideration, added to the other arguments on which I have insisted, make my thoughts so easy on this most interesting question, that I can scarcely wish for more satisfaction.

I will now request leave to add a few observations to guard you against mif-
ap-

apprehensions of God's goodness, after which I will proceed to an account of some of the principal effects of it, and the influence which the belief of it ought to have on our tempers and practises.

I have already observed, that the goodness of God is not to be considered as a propensity in him of which no account can be given, and which produces its effects necessarily. On the contrary; I have shewn, that it is implied in the perfect intelligence of the Deity; and that it is to be considered as under the direction of reason, and as always operating, though *certainly*, yet *freely*.

It follows from hence, that we should consider it as a holy and just goodness. This observation appears to me of particular importance. If it is not remembered, we shall be in danger of entertaining very groundless expectations from this attribute. God's goodness, when moral agents are considered as the objects of it, is not a difposition to make all happy indifcriminately at any rate and by any means. Were this true, it would not be an excellence becoming the dignity and wifdom of a Being perfectly reafonable. —On the contrary; it is a difposition to make the upright and worthy happy, preferably to others. It is a principle which, in all its exertions, is directed by a regard to rectitude, and an averfion to moral evil. The end of it is, indeed, happinefs. But it is the *righteft* happinefs. It is happinefs enjoyed in the practice of virtue.

In connexion with this, I would obferve that our expectations from God's goodnefs fhould be regulated by what we fee to be the eftablifhed order of nature. This, in all cafes, is the beft guide of our expectations and reafonings.—We are, in the higheft degree, incompetent judges of the method in which Divine goodnefs ought to purfue its end, and it is prefumptuous and foolifh to lay a ftrefs, in this

this case, on any theories that we can form. We are no less unqualified for *governing* worlds than we are for *making* them; and yet this is what, in our vain imaginations, we are continually doing. Let us study to acquire a juster sense of our own insufficiency; and learn to submit our understandings to that Supreme intelligence which includes in it Supreme benevolence, and which, we may assure ourselves, will conduct all events in the best ways to the best issues.—If we will judge by what lies before us, we must be satisfied, that the plan of the Divine government is to make the happiness of reasonable beings to depend on their own endeavours; and also, within certain limits, on the agency and benevolence of their fellow-beings. The chief blessings of existence do not fall to our share of course, without any sollicitude of our own. They are offered to our *acquisition*, not our *acceptance*; and the condition of our *having* them, is our *earning* them by

the

the exercise of the powers given us. Our fellow-creatures, likewise, are often the conveyers of them; and *their* voluntary instrumentality is, in numberless instances, made to be not only the *channel* by which they are communicated, but the *condition* on which they are granted.—There is no part of the constitution of nature that deserves more of our attention than this. Objections to it are apt to rise within us, and we may be ready to ask—" Why does the Deity seem to grudge " us bliss by suspending it on such con-" ditions, and making it so precarious?"—But, in reality, it is an instance of perfect wisdom. The natures of things render this method of treating moral agents necessary; and it is the method of treating them which must in the end produce the greatest good. I have observed this in my former discourse [a], and, therefore, will say no more of it now.

Again;

[a] See, likewise, the fifth of these discourses, page 161, &c.

Again; I would caution you against expecting, that this attribute should, *in every single instance*, produce the greatest possible effect. If we see that happiness is intended and goodness displayed in the frame of the world, we should be satisfied. To complain because *more* happiness has not been produced, and *more* goodness displayed, would be very unreasonable. It would be complaining on a ground not possible to be removed; and giving way to a disposition not possible to be satisfied: For, were the quantity of happiness produced ever so great, there would be still room for more happiness. Had there been never a sigh, a pang or a groan on this earth, we might have imagined that there should have been higher pleasures enjoyed by its inhabitants; or, at least, that it should have been better stocked and made larger. Had we been happy to the utmost extent of our capacities, we might have thought that we should have had greater capacities; and had we been ANGELS, we might

might have thought that we should have been ARCH-ANGELS.—Away then with all such complaints. If we see God to be good, let us not ask, why he is not better? If we feel that he has made us *happy*, let us not be so ungrateful as to murmur because he has not made us *happier*.—It is probable that, upon the whole, an infinite sum of happiness is produced; but we are by no means judges in what degree it ought to be produced in particular instances. The goodness of God, like all his other attributes, must, in many respects, be incomprehensible to us. We do not know (as I have already intimated) what measures are best to be pursued, or what laws are best to be established, in order to gain its ends most effectually and completely. General regulations may be necessary which may sometimes produce great calamities; and executions of justice may be proper which may appear to us severe. Let us never forget our own ignorance. There is no topick from which we are apt to argue more wantonly than from God's goodnefs. It would be ftrange, indeed, if we could difcover how the affairs of the world ought to be adminiftered; or if beings, with our narrow views, were to meet with no difficulties in contemplating the meafures taken by Infinite Wifdom to bring about infinite happinefs.

Again; we muft conceive of the goodnefs of God as impartial and univerfal. It does not arbitrarily diftinguifh fome from others, without regarding reafon and fitnefs. It has no favourites, except fuch moral agents as beft practife righteoufnefs. It flows in numberlefs ftreams to all living beings, according to their different capacities. It has produced innumerable worlds which it continually fupports and maintains. It fhines through all nature. It embraces and bleffes the whole creation.

Once more. It is immutable and everlafting. It can never fail or change. It has

has exifted *from* eternity, and it will continue *to* eternity; ftill flowing, and yet never exhaufted; ftill giving, and yet having infinitely more to give; the fpring of all other goodnefs, and the caufe of all order, joy, and perfection.

But thefe obfervations anticipate the account which I have propofed to give of fome of the chief effects of Divine goodnefs. This reprefentation muft be brief and extremely defective; but it will anfwer my intention, fhould it be the means of leading you, for a few moments, to attend a little more clofely to this fubject; and to join with me in endeavouring to awaken our gratitude to the Deity, by recollecting carefully, on this occafion, what it is we owe to him.

A profpect here offers itfelf to us the moft delightful.—All nature replenifhed with the effects of uncreated and everlafting goodnefs! An univerfe boundlefs in extent, and to which all that we can imagine

imagine is nothing, built on purpofe to be the feat of blifs! Myriads of ftarry worlds, and countlefs hofts of living beings, brought forth by one munificent Parent to partake of his bounty; all dependent on his providence, fupported by his power, and provided for by his care and love!—With what admiration muft we reflect on the wife and good order of that fyftem to which we belong? How does it declare, as far as we can carry our views, the benevolence of its Omnipotent Maker? Every region of this earth we fee abounding with inhabitants; and fo overflowing is Divine goodnefs in this part of nature, that it has brought into exiftence every different kind and form of animal life that we can conceive to be poffible. There is no chafm in the chain of being from reafoning man down to the inanimate vegetable. Every rivulet, every leaf, and almoft every atom of matter about us is peopled. What then muft we think of the furrounding planets? Are not they

they alſo ſtocked with a like variety of happy inhabitants? If on this earth the Parent of all has been ſo munificent, what nobler ſcenes of being and bliſs may we ſuppoſe to be exhibited in the remoter diſtricts of the creation?—But let us confine our thoughts to thoſe objects which are moſt near and familiar to us.

It has been juſt obſerved, that every region of the earth abounds with inhabitants, and that no order of beings below man ſeems here to have been left unproduced. The ſea and the rivers are ſtored with numberleſs tribes of creatures, who have organs adapted to their reſpective exigencies and places of reſidence. The dry land is appropriated to other orders of beings, who have alſo the beſt proviſion made for their ſubſiſtence and preſervation. The air, likewiſe, has its proper animals of various kinds that cut their way through it, and are furniſhed with ſuitable powers and faculties. All theſe diſcover ſigns of happineſs. They diſplay

play the exuberant goodness of their Maker. He maketh his sun to shine upon them; and continually feeds, protects, and cherishes them.—*He sendeth the springs into the valleys which run among the hills. By them the fowls of heaven have their habitation which sing among the branches. He causes the grass to grow for cattle, and herbs for the service of man. He maketh the darkness and it is night, wherein all the beasts of the forest do creep forth. The young lions roar after their prey, and ask their meat of God. The sun ariseth; they gather themselves together, and lie down in their dens. The earth is full of his riches. So is the great and wide sea, wherein are creatures-innumerable. These all wait upon him. That which he giveth them, they gather. He openeth his hand, and they are filled with good.* Pf. civ.

But let us fix our thoughts particularly on MAN.—The flightest examination will convince us, that we are indeed wonderful instances of the goodness of our Maker.
Every

Every circumstance of our situation, and every power of our minds affords us some proof of this. By the various degrees of enjoyment arising from the senses and appetites of the lower part of our natures, we are enabled to conceive what the enjoyment is of the creatures below us. But we have many sources of happiness greatly superior to any they possess.—We have powers of IMAGINATION, by which we are rendered capable of the pleasures arising from the perception of harmony, order, and beauty. — We have MEMORY, by which we are able to recall and revive past scenes and enjoyments.—We have a capacity of looking forward to futurity; and thus of guarding against expected evils, and of alleviating present inconveniences by the anticipations of HOPE.—We have LANGUAGE, by which we can make known our thoughts to one another, and enjoy the benefits of social intercourse and communication. — We have PUBLIC AFFECTIONS, which prompt us to pursue the

the happiness of our fellow-men, and furnish us with the joys flowing from love and sympathy; from friendship, generosity, and mutual kindness.—We have REASON, by which we can investigate truth, see the hand that formed us, contemplate his works, and cause all nature about us and every inferior order of beings to contribute to our defence and comfort.—We have LIBERTY and CONSCIENCE, by which we can perceive the eternal differences of moral good and evil; and, by conforming our actions to them, procure the inexpressible satisfaction arising from self-applause, the consciousness of imitating the Deity, and the hope of his approbation and favour.

These are some of the distinguishing privileges which place us at the head of this world, and lay the foundation of our peculiar happiness.—It is true, each of them may, through our folly, become the cause of evil to us. But such evils must not be charged on our Maker,

Maker. The unhappiness we bring upon ourselves by misconduct, it would be wicked to impute to him. Our crimes are no part of his constitution. The powers with which we are endowed were designed to be advantages to us, though we often turn them into occasions of mischief. Liberty, language, and reason are the greatest blessings, though they often produce, in consequence of our perverseness, distresses and calamities. We should learn to judge of every gift and appointment of the Deity by its essential tendencies and general effects, and not by any incidental consequences arising from them. —Who can doubt but that fire, air, and water, are unspeakable benefits, though sometimes they break out into conflagrations, deluges, and hurricanes?— In truth, we may read the goodness of the Creator in the evils as well as the blessings of life. These evils are either kind provisions against greater evils; or the result of laws necessary to the being of the world,

world, and useful in their design and operation.—I made this observation in my last discourse, and endeavoured to explain and illustrate it. It is an observation on which great stress has been justly laid by all the best writers on this subject.

The tragical events in human life produced by ungoverned passions, by the abuse of reason, and other causes, are, without doubt, very shocking. But I seldom feel myself moved by them to question the goodness of God. What makes such events impress us so much is, their being out of the ordinary course of things. We generally see that they take their rise from a wise and kind constitution; and if, in any instance, we cannot see this, they are only single facts standing in opposition to millions.—Look at that man who has ruined his fortune and broken his health by his vices. Can you be disposed to censure the Creator on his account? Or would you have had him make the world in such a manner as that wickedneſs ſhould have gone unreſtrained and unpuniſhed?—Had this been done, you would indeed have had reaſon to doubt his goodneſs.

Look at another perſon who is now curſing his exiſtence under the miſery of a diſordered imagination, and the deſpair and horrors of a deep melancholy. You cannot but view him with compaſſion, and think his caſe ſhocking. But conſider that it is not likely *you* can be better than the Being who gave you your compaſſion. Conſider, likewiſe, that perhaps this perſon has, in former life, enjoyed more happineſs than is equivalent to his preſent ſufferings; and that, in future life, he may again be happy, and find reaſon to be thankful for what he now endures. Suppoſe, however, the worſt. His caſe is plainly ſingular. Had God intended miſery, we ſhould all of us have been ſuch wretched beings.

But to return to the account I was attempting to give you of the effects of God's goodneſs to us.

It

It was God that raised us out of nothing, and brought us forth to enjoy the light of life, and to view this glorious theatre of nature. To him we owe these thoughts that wander through eternity; and those high faculties by which we claim kindred with angels, and which qualify us for acting by the same rule with him, and for loving, serving, and adoring him.—It is he that continually preserves and maintains us: Without him we cannot subsist one moment. Every breath we draw; every step we take; every thought we think depends entirely upon him. Every place we are in, and every instant of our duration is crouded with his mercies. It is his raiment cloaths us, and his food that nourishes us. It is he that shelters us in our houses, refreshes us in sleep, watches over us in danger, and defends us against the evils to which we are exposed. It is he that supplies our returning wants, that chears our hearts among our friends, and that delights us in every agreeable object and scene. From him we derive every gratification which we receive by our senses; every benefit we owe to our fellow-creatures; every hope that expands our breasts; and every convenience which renders our lives comfortable. There is, in short, no advantage which we can procure for ourselves, no joy that springs up in our hearts, no blessing that crowns our existence, which does not come from him the Giver of every good and perfect gift. —He takes care of us at those seasons when we are incapable of taking any care of ourselves. He dispenses blessings to us when we cannot reflect whence they come; and, in numberless instances, goes before our wishes, and *prevents* us with his benefits.—He follows, with his goodness, even the wicked and undeserving. The most inexcusable ingratitude cannot easily divert its course. His hand upholds and conducts us when we are so blind and insensible as not to acknowledge it. He promotes the happiness of those base people who can spend their days without addressing any acts of homage to him, or ever thinking of worshipping and thanking him. *He does good to the evil and unthankful, and sends his rain on the just and the unjust*, Mat. v. 45.

Above all things; he has blest us with the Gospel, and sent Jesus Christ to save us. This was an instance of goodness to sinful creatures which exceeds all our comprehension.—When mankind had corrupted their ways, and lost the knowledge of the one true God, Jesus Christ descended from heaven to call them back to their duty, and to redeem them from all iniquity. *This is love*, the Scriptures tell us, *not that we loved God, but that he loved us, and sent his Son to be the propitiation for our sins.*—In consequence of that fall, or degradation of man, related in the book of Genesis, and referred to throughout all the subsequent parts of the Bible, we had lost immortality, and became subject to that evil of death which we have all of us in prospect. And it is impossible to say what this would have been to us, had not Infinite Goodness provided for us a Saviour who, by giving himself up to death, has delivered us from death, restored us to our forfeited happiness, and laid a foundation for the exercise of full favour to all true penitents. By giving us Christ, God has, indeed, given us every thing necessary to raise us to the highest dignity and glory—the clearest light—the best account of our duty—the strongest motives to right practice—great and precious promises—and, particularly, the promise of a resurrection from death to a new life of endless bliss, in that future kingdom of Jesus Christ, into which will be gathered all the virtuous and worthy among mankind.

Such are the effects of the goodness of God to us; such the blessings we owe to him.—I must add, that our sense of these blessings will be rendered more intense,
if

if we can reflect that we have duly improved them, and been led by them to true piety and righteousness. To this important end he conducts us by every proper method; urging us by his authority; inviting us by his promises; admonishing us by the remonstrances of ministers and friends; assisting us by his grace; and sparing us from year to year with much patience and long-suffering. And when, in consequence of these advantages, we have been engaged to resolve upon amendment, and to begin a life of virtue, he continues his grace and influence to carry us on in our course, and to promote our endeavours after constant improvement, till we are taken out of this world to receive our reward.—But what will this reward be?—What is the happiness reserved for all the upright and virtuous?—No language can describe this. No imagination is capable of conceiving it. *Be glad in the Lord, ye righteous; and shout for joy, all ye who are upright in heart.*

heart. All have reaſon to be thankful for exiſtence; but you have reaſon for exultation and triumph. Your happineſs will never come to an end. It is to be renewed in brighter regions, and there to go on increaſing to all eternity. While you continue in this world the preſence of God is always with you, and nothing amiſs can happen to you. And when you have finiſhed your courſe here, you will be taken to that world where all tears will be wiped away from your eyes; where the hand of death ſhall never again reach you; where you ſhall join ſuperior beings, and be for ever improving under the eye and care of the Almighty.—This will be the finiſhing effect of God's goodneſs to mankind; and to this iſſue of all preſent events no one of us can fail attaining who does not render himſelf unfit for it, and unworthy of it by vicious practices and habits.

The practical improvement of this ſubject is very obvious.

Firſt.

First. It has a tendency to fix our minds in a state of tranquillity and satisfaction. Did blind fate, or fickle fortune, or a relentless tyrant govern all things, our condition would be deplorable. We could consider no object with pleasure, and all about us would appear dark and desolate. But we are infinitely happier. Perfect goodness is at the head of the world; and, therefore, all may be expected to take place in it that the most benevolent mind can desire.

Secondly; It is obvious, that the goodness of God is the proper object of our warmest praises. We must be lost in insensibility, if we can contemplate it without feeling ourselves prompted to adoration and thankfgiving. What can engage our gratitude and love, if original and sovereign goodness will not?—There is no property of our natures by which we are more distinguished from the creatures below us, than the capacity of seeing and acknowledging God's goodness. How shocking

shocking then are the characters of those men who discover no sense of it; and who (though they live by the Deity and depend every instant on his care) yet willingly forget him, and neglect all religious worship? What can be more shameful; or shew a heart more void of just feelings and sentiments? Ingratitude is one of the basest vices; and, certainly, ingratitude to the best of Beings cannot be less base than any other kind of ingratitude. On the contrary; he ought to be the *first* object of our gratitude, and a disposition to acknowledge him in all our ways ought to be the governing principle within us.—Nothing bestows more dignity on a character than an unaffected and ardent piety; nor is any thing more reasonable and becoming. But how little of it do we see?—I have just said, that the capacity of acknowledging the Deity is one of our chief distinctions from the lower animals; but multitudes about us chuse to give up this distinction. They can

can enjoy the bleſſings of life without lifting up their ſouls to the donor of them. They can think of the Being who is the cauſe of all joy and the fountain of all good without being kindled into devotion.

Thirdly; The goodneſs of God ſhews us the folly and baſeneſs of ſin. All moral evil is an abuſe of the love, and diſobedience to the authority, of that Being who is always doing us good, and whoſe character comprehends in it every excellence which can be a reaſon for affection and veneration. It is ſlighting and offending our beſt Benefactor, and turning the very bleſſings we derive from him into inſtruments of oppoſition to him.—Had we a juſt ingenuity of temper, nothing would have a ſtronger tendency to produce in us a deep contrition for our ſins, than the reflexion, that by them we have counteracted and affronted perfect goodneſs; nor would any thing impreſs us more in favour of virtue, than the conſideration that it is a concurrence with the views of Infinite

finite Goodnefs, and that by it we pleafe and obey our all-benevolent Parent and Preferver. If we feel that we are not influenced by confiderations of this kind, we want one of the moft proper fprings of virtue, and we may be fure that our characters are fadly defective.

Farther. The goodnefs of God ought to be imitated by us. It cannot but be his will that we fhould be merciful as he is merciful, and do good to one another as he does good to us all. It fhould be our ambition to act thus; and, as far as poffible, to employ our little power in the fame manner that God employs his unlimited power. No being can have a higher or nobler ambition.—What gives luftre to all God's attributes is his goodnefs. This chiefly is the excellence that makes him amiable. He has given us the power of acquiring fome degree of the fame excellence. Let us not neglect or abufe fo tranfporting a privilege of our natures. Let us ftrive to copy into our own hearts the

the benevolence of our Maker, by cultivating in ourselves every kind affection, and studying to relieve the pains and to increase the happiness of all about us. Thus shall we be his genuine offspring, and secure his particular favour and protection.

Lastly. The goodness of God should engage us to put our trust in him. I am led particularly to observe this by the latter part of the verse I have taken for my text —*Oh! taste and see that the Lord is good. Blessed is the man that trusteth in him.*— God made us to make us happy. He directs all events in the best manner, and for the best purposes. The whole creation is his family, over which he is continually watching. Innumerable beings are every moment brought forth by him to exist for ever the objects of his liberality. With what confidence should we commit our whole existence to this Being, and give up ourselves to his disposal? How should the reflexion that he reigns

revive

revive our hearts, and diffipate our anxieties? What may we not hope for from his boundlefs goodnefs? How fafe are all our interefts under his management?—Let us, however, take care not to forget an obfervation which was made at the beginning of this difcourfe. Let us remember, that our expectations from God ought to be regulated by a regard to his JUSTICE. Though he loves his creatures, he muft hate the wicked. Sin is the fubverfion of that order, and an oppofition to thofe laws by which the world fubfifts; and, for this reafon, even goodnefs requires that it fhould be punifhed, and that virtue fhould be made the univerfal ground and condition of happinefs. An ill man, therefore, can build no hopes on the goodnefs of God. To truft in him at the fame time that we counteract his will and live in guilt, would be a wretched folly and prefumption.

But to conclude the whole.—Let us, with one heart, give glory to God, and
cele-

celebrate his praises. Let us rejoice in his government, and never shrink from any thing our duty to him requires. Let us love him with all our souls and with all our strength, and let our love to him shew itself by loving all his creatures.—His mercies are more than we can number; and it is not possible for us to make him any adequate returns.—*Oh! sing unto the Lord a new song.* (Psal. ciii.) *Sing unto the Lord all the earth. Sing unto the Lord. Bless his name. Shew forth his salvation from day to day. Give unto the Lord the glory due unto his name. Say among the Heathen that the Lord reigneth.—Let the heavens rejoice, and the earth be glad. Let the fields be joyful, and all that is therein. For the Lord is good; his mercy is from everlasting, and his truth endureth to all generations.—Bless the Lord ye his angels that excel in strength. Bless the Lord all ye his hosts; ye ministers of his that do his pleasure. Bless the Lord all his works in all places of his dominions.*

dominions—Let the whole creation join in raising a song of praise to him.—*Bless the Lord, Oh! my soul.*

SERMON X.

OF THE RESURRECTION OF LAZARUS.

JOHN xi. 43, 44.

And when he had thus spoken, he cried with a loud voice, LAZARUS, COME FORTH. *And he that was dead came forth bound hand and foot with grave-clothes. And his face was bound about with a napkin. Jesus says to them; Loose him, and let him go.*

MY design from these words, is to make a few observations on the miraculous fact related in them. This is one of the most remarkable of all our Saviour's miracles. It is related by the Apostle

Apostle John with a simplicity of style; and the main circumstances attending it are told with a minuteness, and, at the same time, a brevity, that cannot but impress an unprejudiced mind. Had a person who knew he was endeavouring to gain belief to an imposition which he had been concerned in contriving, given us this narrative, it would have been told in a very different manner. It would, probably, have been drawn out to a greater length. No particular mention would have been made of times, places, and persons; and some affected apologies and colourings would have been introduced to give it plausibility, and to guard against objections. But, instead of this, we find it a narrative plain and artless in the highest degree, without a circumstance that shews an attempt to give it any dress, or an expression that betrays a design to surprize and deceive. In short; the astonishing miracle which is the subject of this narrative, is told us exactly as we
should

should expect an honest but unlettered man, who had been familiarized to miracles, to relate a fact of this kind, to which he was conscious of having been an eye and ear witness.

It has been thought strange that the other Evangelists have omitted to give us an account of this miracle. Several reasons have been assigned for this omission, which I will just mention to you.

It should be considered, that none of the Evangelists appear to have aimed at giving us a complete account of all our Saviour's miracles. It should be considered farther, that this miracle was performed in the interval of time between our Saviour's going into the country beyond Jordon, and his going up to his last passover; and that this was a more private part of his ministry, concerning which the other Evangelists have said little. But what deserves most to be attended to is, that the Evangelists must have felt a particular delicacy with respect to the publication of this miracle. First; because it was a miracle performed on a *friend* in a family with which our Saviour was intimate. And secondly; because Lazarus might be still living at the time they wrote their Gospels, and might be subjected to great inconveniences by having his name mentioned as the subject of such a miracle. This, however, was a reason which cannot be supposed to have existed when John wrote. There was a tradition among the Fathers, that *Lazarus* lived thirty years after his resurrection; and John did not write his Gospel till at least forty or fifty years afterwards. Lazarus, therefore, most probably was not then alive; and John, for this reason, must have been more at liberty to give an account of his resurrection.

It seems proper farther to mention here, that St. John, as he wrote last, wrote also on purpose to give a supplement to the other Gospels. He had read these Gospels,

pels, and finding that some important particulars were omitted in them, and others not fully enough related, he composed *his* Gospel to supply their defects. John's Gospel will appear particularly striking when viewed in this light. Whoever will compare it with the other Gospels must find, that he is generally careful to avoid repeating accounts which the other Evangelists had given before him; and that the bulk of it is a relation of facts and instructions about which they have been silent. The account I am now to consider is one instance of this. Tho' extremely short, considering the magnitude of the fact, it is given us more fully than most of the accounts of Christ's other miracles; and we cannot employ ourselves more profitably than in considering it.

What may be first worth your notice in this miracle, is the character of the person on whom it was performed. Our Saviour

Saviour had a particular affection for him. He calls him his *friend* in the 11th verse of this chapter; and the message which was sent him to acquaint him with his illness was expressed in these words: *Lord, Behold he whom thou lovest is sick.* We may well believe, that a person who was thus distinguished, must have been endowed with some very amiable qualities. John tells us farther, that he had two sisters, whose names were *Martha* and *Mary*; and that they lived together in a village called *Bethany*, within fifteen furlongs of Jerusalem. When Lazarus was taken ill, our Saviour was at a considerable distance from *Bethany*. It was natural for *Martha* and *Mary*, knowing the particular affection he had for their brother, to hope that he would exert those miraculous powers by which he had cured others, in recovering this his *friend*. They, therefore, sent to him to inform him of their brother's sickness, hoping that he would soon come to them, and
give

give them relief. But, we are told, that, after receiving the message, he staid *two days* in the place where he was. The reason of this delay was, that he chose Lazarus should die before he got to *Bethany*, because he intended, for the fuller manifestation of his Divine Mission, to raise him from the dead. Had he been on the spot when Lazarus died, he would have suffered, perhaps, some troublesome importunities; nor, I think, would it have looked so well for him to have permitted Lazarus to die while he was with him, and after that to raise him from the dead.

Secondly; The humility which our Lord discovered on this occasion is worth our notice. After staying two days where he was when he received the account of Lazarus's sickness, he told his disciples that he was resolved to go into *Judea*, and invited them to go with him, informing them, at the same time, of the death of Lazarus. The words in which he gave this information are a little remarkable. Ver. 11. *Our friend Lazarus sleepeth, and I go to awake him out of sleep.* He does not say, *Lazarus is dead.* That would have been too harsh. Nor does he say; *I go to raise him from the dead, and thus to display my great power.* A deceiver would, probably, have used some boasting language of this kind. But he, avoiding all oftentation, expresses himself in the gentlest and simplest language, saying only, " that Lazarus was *asleep*, and that he was going to *wake* him."—Another circumstance to the same purpose, is his ordering the stone to be removed from the mouth of the sepulchre just before he ordered Lazarus to come forth. He might, undoubtedly, have commanded the stone to roll away of itself; and, perhaps, a bold impostor would have been represented as doing this. But our Lord did not multiply miracles needlessly, or do any thing for the sake only of shew and parade.—Again; the manner in which he refers

refers this miracle to the will and power of God requires our attention. After the stone was taken away, he made, we are told, a solemn addrefs to God; and, lifting up his eyes, said, *Father, I thank thee that thou haft heard me.* This implies, that his ability to work this miracle was the confequence of his having prayed for it. Throughout his whole miniftry, he was careful to direct the regards of men to the Deity, as the fountain of all his powers. His language was; *The Father who dwelleth in me, he doth the works. I can of mine own felf do nothing. I came to do the will of him that fent me.*

Thirdly; We fhould take notice in the account of this miracle, of the tendernefs and benevolence of our Saviour's difpofition. It is faid, that when he faw Mary weeping, and the Jews alfo weeping, he groaned in his fpirit, and was troubled. And it is added, as a circumftance particularly obfervable, that HE likewife wept. JESUS WEPT. Ver. 35. The remarks which.

which, we are told, the spectators made on this, are very natural. Some, imagining that his tears flowed from his concern for the death of his friend, said, *Behold how he loved him.* Others, wondering that, as Lazarus was his friend, he had not exerted the miraculous powers by which he had cured others in curing him, said; *Could not this man who opened the eyes of the blind, have caused that even this man should not have died?* Ver. 37.—The reason of his weeping could not be his sorrow for the death of Lazarus; for he well knew that he should soon restore him to life: but, most probably, his sympathy with the sorrow of Lazarus's friends, heightened by reflexions, to which on this occasion he might be led, on death and its attendant evils. He might, likewise, be much impressed (as we find he was at other times) by observing the perverseness discovered by some of the Jews who surrounded him, and by his foresight of the calamities that threatened them. We have an an account of his weeping on another occasion in Luke xix. 41. where it is said, that when he came near to *Jerusalem* and beheld it, he *wept* over it. In these instances we see plainly the workings of an ardent benevolence; and we may infer from them, that it is by no means below the character of a wise man to be, on certain occasions, so far overcome by his affectionate feelings, as to be forced into tears. This happened to our Saviour on the occasions I have mentioned; and he only appears to us the more amiable for it. Wretched, indeed, is that philosophy which teaches us to suppress our tender feelings. Such a philosophy, by aiming at elevating us above human nature, sinks us below it. Our Saviour was greater than any human being; and yet we find that even he wept. How foolish then would it be in us to be ashamed of any similar tenderness into which we may be forced? A stoical insensibility is certainly rather a vice than a virtue. At no time does a person

person appear more lovely than when conquered by his kind affections, and melted by them into tears. Let us then learn to despise all pretensions to a wisdom which would take from us any of our natural sensibilities; remembering, however, to take care to keep them always, as far as we can, under proper restraint. It is neither a sin nor a weakness to fall into tears; but it is wrong to weep like persons who have no hope, or who are not satisfied with God's will. Our passions have been wisely and kindly given us; and our duty is, not to eradicate but to regulate them, by so watching over them as never to suffer them to lead us into any excesses that would betray an impotence of mind, and a diffidence of Providence.

Fourthly; The DIGNITY of Christ in working this miracle deserves our attention. How great did he appear in his conversation with Martha before he got to the sepulchre; and, particularly, when he he declared of himself that he was the RESURRECTION and the LIFE, and that *he who believeth in him, though he were dead, yet shall he live?* How great did he appear when, after addressing himself to the Deity, he cried out with a loud voice at the sepulchre, LAZARUS COME FORTH? And when, in consequence of this call, *Lazarus* immediately awoke from death, and shewed himself in perfect health? What a manifestation was this of his glory, and how evidently did it prove that the power of God dwelt in him?

But this leads me to desire you to attend to the assurance this miracle gives us of the Divine mission of Christ. We can scarcely conceive of a more wonderful exertion of power, than the instantaneous restoration to life and health of a person whose body was putrifying in the grave. He that did this must have been sent of God. It is wholly inconceivable, that a deceiver should be able to produce such credentials. It is only the power

which

which gave life that can thus restore it, and re-unite our souls and bodies after a separation. We may, therefore, assure ourselves, that the person who worked this miracle, and who possessed such an absolute command over nature as Christ discovered, was indeed what he declared himself to be, a Messenger from heaven to save mankind, and that great Messiah whose coming had been promised from the beginning of the world.

It has been urged by unbelievers, that, granting the reality of miracles, they are no proof of the truth of doctrines, there being no connexion between a display of supernatural power and truth. The stress which unbelievers have laid on this objection is mere affectation. Did they believe the miracles, they would, whatever they may pretend, find themselves under a necessity of receiving the doctrines of Christianity; and, it will be time enough to answer this objection, when a man can be found, not a lunatic, who can honestly

nestly say, that he believes the miracle in particular which is the subject of this discourse, but does not believe the doctrine which it was intended to prove.

But what deserves more particular notice here is, that it appears from this miracle, that Christ is hereafter to raise all mankind from death. Just before he performed it, *Martha* having said to him, *Lord if thou hadst been here, my brother had not died*, he told her, in order to comfort her, that her brother should rise again. She, not understanding him, replied, *I know that he shall rise again at the resurrection at the last day*; to which he answered, with a voice of unspeakable dignity, *I am the* RESURRECTION *and the* LIFE. *He that believeth in me, though he were dead, yet shall he live: and whosoever liveth and believeth in me shall never die.* That is, " I am the person by whom mankind are " to be raised from the dead. It signifies " not whether he that is my true disciple " is dead or alive. If he is *dead*, he shall
" live

" live again ; and if he is *alive*, his exift-
" ence fhall be continued to him beyond
" the grave, and his difmiffion from this
" world fhall be his introduction to a
" better world, where he fhall never
" die."— After making this declaration,
and to demonftrate the truth of it by
giving a *fpecimen* of that power by which
he was to effect the univerfal refurrection,
he walked to Lazarus's grave, and raifed
him from the dead.—What evidence could
be more decifive?—We have in the Gofpel
Hiftory, accounts of his raifing from the
dead two other perfons; and, after being
crucified and buried, he rofe himfelf from
the dead and afcended to heaven.—Thefe
facts exhibit him to our fenfes as indeed
the RESURRECTION and the LIFE. No
doubt can remain of a doctrine thus proved.
—Give me leave to hold your attention
here a little longer.——In John v. 25,
our Saviour, we are told, faid to the Jews,
*Verily, verily, I fay unto you, the hour is
coming, and* NOW IS, *when the dead fhall
hear*

hear the voice of the Son of God, and they that hear shall live. Soon after uttering these words, he said again, as we read in the same chapter, verse 28. *The hour is coming when all that are in their graves shall hear the voice of the Son of Man, and shall come forth. They that have done good to the resurrection of life; and they that have done evil to the resurrection of damnation.*

In the circumstances which attended the resurrection of Lazarus, our Saviour seems to have referred to these declarations, and to have intended to verify and exemplify them. He cried, we are told, ver. 43, with a loud voice, like, perhaps, to that by which he had said he would hereafter raise all the dead, LAZARUS, *come forth*; and in a moment he did come forth.— Thus will the whole world at the last day hear the voice of the Son of God. Thus will he then burst the bars of the grave, rescue from the king of terrors his prisoners, and call to life the dead of all nations,

tions, ranks, and times.—How awful this prospect? How consoling and elevating to good men, amidst the waste that death is continually making around them?—— What reason have we to value our relation to that Deliverer to whom, under God, it is owing? And how ought we to triumph in the assurance he has given us, that, though we must soon lose our powers in death, we shall hereafter recover them: spring up from the dust at his command, new made and improved; and, with all the faithful, enter (not on such a life as that to which *Lazarus* was restored) but on a glorious and endless life in the heavens?

Before I proceed [a] I shall here request your attention, while I briefly consider the objections which unbelievers have made to the account given by St. John of this miracle. Sufficient notice has been already taken of several of these objections;

---

[a] Here this sermon was divided into two sermons.

tions; but there are some which have not been mentioned, and on which it will not be improper to make a few remarks.

It has been asked, whether there is sufficient reason to believe, that *Lazarus* was *really dead*. The answer is, that he died, not *suddenly*, but of an illness that increased gradually, and lasted several days—that, in this case, there is no danger of mistaking the signs of death—that his friends had buried him; and, therefore, must have assured themselves of his death—that he had been in his grave four days; and that, had he not been dead, the napkin which, we are told, was tied round his face, and the grave cloths and filletings with which he was bound, would alone have been sufficient to kill him.

It has been farther enquired, how, if he was bound hand and foot, as St. John tells us, he could, on our Saviour's call, come forth out of the grave. The answer is obvious. Upon the supposition of the reality of the miracle, there can be no difficulty in conceiving it carried so far, as not only to bring *Lazarus* to life, but to present him also out of the grave before the spectators. But were it necessary to suppose the miracle not carried thus far, the objection would deserve little regard, because founded on an ignorance of the manner of burying among the antients. The graves among the Jews and other nations in former times, were caves hewn out of rocks, in the sides of which the dead, after being embalmed, were deposited without coffins. When, therefore, by our Saviour's order, the stone was taken away from the mouth of Lazarus's sepulchre, it is possible that his corpse might be exposed to view; and when it is said, that he *came forth bound hand and foot*, the meaning may be, not that he walked out of the sepulchre; but that he raised himself up in the side of the cave or cell where he was laid, and slid down from it upon his feet, and there con-

continued till he was unbound and could walk about.

But the chief difficulty which occurs in confidering the account of this miracle is, the effect which, we are told, it had on the chief priefts and Pharifees. Inftead of being properly impreffed by it, we read, verfe 53, that, after taking counfel together, they determined to ufe all poffible means to put Jefus to death. They even went fo far as to think of meafures for putting *Lazarus* himfelf to death. Similar to this, according to the Gofpel Hiftory, was the general conduct of the leading Jews with refpect to our Lord. Inftead of being engaged by the increafing glory of his character, and the overpowering evidence of his miracles, to ftrike to him, they were only ftimulated to greater rage, and made more defperate in their refolution to crufh him: And this may feem a pitch of wickednefs fo diabolical as to exceed the limits of human depravity, and, therefore, to be incredible. I am in hopes,

hopes, however, that you will think otherwise, when you have attended to the following observations.

It is a previous observation necessary to be attended to, that the Jewish rulers appear to have been convinced of the supernatural power and prophetical character of our Lord. This the Gospel History plainly tells us. John xii. 42. *Among the chief rulers also many believed on him; but did not confess him, because they loved the praise of men more than the praise of God. We know*, says Nicodemus (the ruler who came to Jesus by night) *that thou art a teacher come from God, for no one can do the miracles thou dost except God be with him.* John iii. 2. On hearing the report of this miracle in particular, the language of the chief priests and Pharisees was; *What do we? for this man doth many miracles. If we let him thus alone, all men will believe in him.* John xi. 47. When we read, that they did *not* believe in him, the meaning is, that they did not *receive* him and

and *submit* to him as a messenger from heaven; and what, therefore, is to be accounted for is, not so much their want of faith in him, as their rejection and persecution of him notwithstanding their faith.

In order to explain this, I would desire you to consider,

First, The general character of the Jews. In every age they had been infamous for their persecution of the prophets who were sent to them. About this time, more especially, it appears that they were arrived at a pitch of wickedness which went beyond common depravity. *Josephus* says, that he believed "there never existed, from the beginning of the world, a generation of men more profligate than the body of the Jewish leaders and nobility were at the time Jerusalem was besieged by the Romans:" And if they were then so vicious, it is not likely they were of a different character forty years before, when our Lord preached to them.

Secondly; The provocation our Lord gave them should be considered. It is remarkable, that it does not appear that he ever expressed himself with particular warmth except when he spoke of these men. Against the Scribes and Pharisees we find him always declaring a most pointed and irreconcilable indignation. He charged them with being guilty of almost every vice that could stain a human character; and, particularly, with religious hypocrisy, doing all their good works to be seen of men; pretending uncommon sanctity, and making long prayers, but devouring widows houses; straining at a gnat, but swallowing a camel; careful not to omit any punctilio of a ceremony, and paying tithe of mint, anise, and cummin, but neglecting the weightier matters of the law, justice, mercy, and fidelity; binding heavy burthens on others which they would not touch with one

one of their fingers; compassing sea and land to make one proselyte, who, when made, became tenfold more a child of hell than themselves; claiming an absolute authority over the consciences of the people, while they taught for doctrines the commandments of men, and corrupted the law of God; loving greetings in the markets, and the chief seats in synagogues, and studying (by going about in long robes, praying in the corners of the streets, sounding a trumpet when they gave alms, and enlarging the borders of their garments) to appear *outwardly* righteous, while *inwardlly* they were like whited sepulchres, full of dead men's bones and of all uncleanness. In short, their character, according to our Lord's representation of it, was completely detestable; and, perhaps, the account we have of it has been providentially given us to prevent our wondering at the violence of their opposition to our Saviour, notwithstanding all they saw and knew of

his

his miraculous powers. He even declared a preference to them of publicans and finners, of thieves and harlots, who, he affured them, were more likely to enter into the kingdom of the Meffiah than they were.

His difcourfe in the 23d chapter of Matthew, is particularly worth your attention on this occafion. In this difcourfe he denounces the judgments of heaven upon them for their wickednefs, calling them blind guides, and a generation of vipers who could not efcape the damnation of hell. He pronounces feven times the words, WOE UNTO YOU SCRIBES AND PHARISEES, HYPOCRITES; and concludes with faying, there was no remedy for them, but that *on them would come all the righteous blood which had been fhed from the beginning of the world*; that is, a punifhment fo dreadful as to bear to be fo expreffed. Thus did he hold them up to public deteftation as enemies to the progrefs of truth and virtue, and a body of pious knaves deftined to deftruction:

And

And the effect must have been the ruin of their credit and authority. Could there have been a provocation more intolerable? In truth, the wonder is, that they bore him so long as they did; and the probability is, that they would have brought him to a quicker end, had it not been for an awe produced in their minds by the splendor of his miracles, united to their apprehensions of danger from the people, who, we are informed, all took him for a prophet and were ready for a revolt in his favour.

But let us farther consider what they must have done, and how much they must have relinquished, had they struck to him. They must have made themselves the disciples of the Son of a Carpenter, followed by twelve mean fishermen, without state or pomp, or even a place in which to lay his head. They must have descended from their seats of power and influence, and placed themselves under the direction of an enemy who had unmasked

masked and exposed them, and from whom they could expect no mercy. But above all, they must have acknowledged themselves the wicked wretches he had declared them to be, and given up their ambition, their hypocrisy, and their vices. Is it strange, that even miracles, whatever conviction they might extort, did not produce this effect? Perhaps, indeed, there is not *now* a country under heaven in which, in similar circumstances, our Lord would not meet with similar treatment. Suppose, for instance, that in ITALY, a prophet was to arise and to go about preaching repentance to the inhabitants; calling them from the worship of the host, of images, the Virgin Mary, and the saints, to the worship of one God; reprobating Popery as a system of superstition and spiritual fraud and domination, injurious to the essential interests of men, by teaching a way of being religious without being virtuous, and of getting to heaven without forsaking vice; and, at the same time,

de-

delivering woes againſt the public teachers and rulers, as hypocritical corrupters of true religion, as ſupporters of idolatry and falſehood, and enemies to the improvement and happineſs of mankind.— Suppoſe, I ſay, this now to happen in ITALY; what can you imagine would be the effect? What evidence would be ſufficient to engage the Pope, the Cardinals, and the different orders of Prieſts, to liſten to ſuch a preacher and acknowledge his authority; to renounce their uſurped honours and dignities; to give up the abuſes to which they owed their wealth and their conſequences, and to reform their doctrine and manners? Would not the whole force of clerical and civil power be exerted to ſilence and cruſh him as ſoon as poſſible? Would miracles themſelves, unleſs employed for the purpoſe of protecting him, long preſerve him? Would he be perfectly ſafe, even in *this* country, were he to come to us and to attack eſtabliſhed corruptions, pro-

voke

voke the vicious in high places, and unmask religious prevaricators, the supporters of abuses, and the enemies of reformation in the manner our Lord did in *Judea*?

The observation I am now making has been verified by the experience of all past ages. Such is the power of criminal prejudices, and such the stubbornness, and often the fury of vicious men interested in maintaining abuses, that reformers, however powerful their admonitions have been and eminent their characters, have seldom long escaped persecution and violent deaths. Provocations unspeakably less than those given to the Jews by our Saviour, have every where produced the same effects. In ATHENS, the poisoning of SOCRATES. In BRITAIN, the burning of CRANMER, LATIMER, RIDLEY, &c.

But this is by no means all that is to be said in answer to the objection I am considering. In our Lord's circumstances
with

with respect to the Jews, there was much that was peculiar, and that can never again exist in any country. In order to understand this, you must recollect, that all the Jews were, in the time of our Saviour, eagerly and impatiently looking for the Messiah promised in their sacred writings; and that the only notion they had of this Messiah was [a], that he would be a temporal prince and a great conqueror, who would come with a train of splendid courtiers and signs in the heavens, set himself at the head of a mighty army, deliver them from the Roman yoke, restore them to their long lost liberty, and elevate them to the sovereignty of the world. Their leading men, in particular, reckoned on being the most favoured men

[a] This opinion was not confined to the Jews. "There had been, Suetonius tells us (Vespas. cap. 4.) THROUGH ALL THE EAST, an ancient and constant expectation, that at that time some one from *Judea* should obtain the empire of the world."

men in his kingdom, on having their consequence among the people confirmed and enlarged, aud enjoying in the greatest abundance pleasures, preferments, honours, and riches. When, therefore, they heard the fame of Jesus, and saw the displays of his supernatural power, they could not but be led to conclude, that he might prove the Messiah, or, at least, that the nation would take him to be so; and, as he had avowed himself their adversary, this would necessarily alarm them. It was impossible they should not dislike *such* a Messiah—a Messiah who was continually warning the people against them, and who had sunk their credit— a Messiah who made humility, self-denial, repentance, and heavenly-mindedness, the conditions of his favour—a Messiah who publicly threatened them, who had pronounced them the worst of mankind, and declared, that instead of sharing in the happiness of the Messiah's reign, they would be excluded from

from it, become victims of Divine justice, and suffer a punishment sharper than any that had been ever inflicted.

It is true that, with wonderful prudence, he avoided declaring himself the Messiah. The effect of such a declaration would have been producing tumults which must have defeated his views. The proper time for this was after his departure from this world, when it would be impossible to mistake it for a call to rebellion. But the rulers of the Jews must have expected, that he would soon quit his reserve, publish his pretensions, and set up his standard; and the more he distinguished himself, the more they must have apprehended, that he might do this with a success that (either by enabling him to execute his threats, or by bringing the Roman power upon them) would occasion their ruin. Thus circumstanced, every miracle he wrought, every testimony he received of popular favour, and every display he made of his prophetical character, could, in their depraved minds have no other effect than to encreafe their alarm, to work them up to greater violence, and to render them more defperate in their attempts to provide for their own fecurity by deftroying him.

Our Lord's parable of the vineyard let out to unfaithful hufbandmen, delivered not long before his crucifixion, affords a particular confirmation of thefe obfervations. In this parable, he intimates to the chief priefts and elders of the people that, in fpite of all their efforts, he fhould rife to univerfal power; and that the confequence would be, his falling upon them (like a great corner-ftone) and grinding them to powder. And we are told, that they underftood his meaning, and were fo exafperated by it, that they endeavoured immediately to feize him, but were deterred by the people. See the 21ft chapter of Matthew, from the 25th verfe to the end.

In short; Jesus, after raising *Lazarus* from the dead, became possest of an influence among the people which would, had he availed himself of it, have been irresistible. They [b] were ripened by it for an insurrection, and the slightest encourage-

[b] The disposition of the Jews at this time to rise in favour of every pretender who offered himself to them as the temporal deliverer they expected in the Messiah, is well known. It was this chiefly, as Josephus says, that produced the war which ruined them; and it was our Lord's disappointing their views, by refusing to be made a king, and suffering himself to be taken and condemned, that made the people turn at last against him.

"The Jewish people (says Dr. Lardner, in his "collection of Jewish and Heathen testimonies to the "truth of Christianity, chap. iii. sect. 7.) had met "with many disappointments from our Lord; and "yet, when he entered into Jerusalem in no greater "state than riding on an ass, they accompanied him "with loud acclamations, saying, *Hosanna to the Son* "*of David. Blessed is the King who cometh in the* "*name of the Lord.* And Jesus, not assuming then "the character of an earthly Prince, was a fresh dis-"appointment to them, and left deep resent-"ments."

ment would have brought them together to fight under him, and to proclaim him their great Meſſiah. The hypocrites who, in the tone and with the authority of a prophet ſent from God, he had *proſcribed*, could not obſerve this without terror. Their danger appeared to be increaſing with every increaſe of his popularity, and growing more imminent in proportion to the proofs he gave of his Divine miſſion. They could not but reckon, that as he roſe they muſt ſink; and that either *he* or *they* muſt periſh. This produced a conteſt ſingular and unparalelled. Our Lord gave it up by yielding to their power. It was a great miſtake to think, that his kingdom was a temporal kingdom, or that he had any worldly views. He did not come for ſlaughter and triumph like the ſavage conquerors of this world, but to ſuffer and to die; and it was neceſſary that his death ſhould be a *public* death. His own reſurrection (the ground

ground of all human hope) could not otherwise have been properly ascertained. He, therefore, made a voluntary surrender of himself to his enemies; and, to fulfil the counsels of Providence [c], submitted to be publicly condemned and crucified.

[c] Their success in taking and condemning him led them to conclude they had obtained a complete victory over him, and delivered themselves from the danger with which he had threatened them. But the events which soon followed proved the contrary. He rose to all power in heaven and earth; and, in a few years after this, sent his armies to destroy these murderers. Vengeance came upon them to the uttermost; and his prophetical denunciations were fully verified.—— *Josephus* tells us, that twelve thousand of the Jewish nobility perished at the siege of *Jerusalem*; that the vengeance of heaven appeared plainly to be upon them; and that, in his opinion, all the calamities which had ever happened to any people from the beginning of the world, were not to be compared with those which befel the Jews at this time. Multitudes, he says, were crucified by the *Romans* before the walls; and so great was the number of those who thus suffered, that room was wanting for crosses, and crosses were wanting for bodies.

These observations seem to be a full answer to the objection I have stated. And they explain what is said in Matth. xxvii. 18. that it was from ENVY the chief priests and Pharisees had delivered him; that is, from a jealousy of his popularity, and a dread of its effects: And, also, what we are told (in a passage already quoted) these chief priests said, on hearing of the resurrection of Lazarus, *What do we? for this man doth many miracles. If we let him thus alone, all men will believe in him, and the Romans will come and take away both our place and nation.* John xi. 47, 48.

There are two reflexions which are naturally suggested to us by these observations.

First; We should consider how striking a proof they give us of the truth of our religion. Had Christ been a deceiver, he would have fallen in with the prejudices of his countrymen. He would have offered himself to them as just the Messiah they expected and wanted; for it was only in the scheme of such a Messiah the views of a deceiver could be gratified. He would have endeavoured to ingratiate himself with the chief priests and rulers, encouraged their ambition, and flattered their vices. You have heard how differently he acted; how he provoked instead of soothing the Jewish rulers, and threatened instead of flattering them; and thus made himself odious and terrible to them in the highest degree. There cannot be a stronger argument for his Divine mission. If there is any person who does not feel the weight of it, he must be either very much prejudiced, or very inattentive.

Secondly; We are led, by the observations I have made, to reflect on the wisdom of Divine Providence, in ordering the circumstances which attended the introduction of Christianity into the world. Had the body of the Jewish leaders and priests (and consequently the nation in general) received Christ, the evidences of our religion would have been much diminished. A suspicion would have been unavoidable, that it was an
im-

impofition contrived by the Jews, and which had made its way in the world by the power and policy [d] of the Jewifh ftate.

But I have gone far beyond the bounds I intended in fpeaking on this fubject.

Let

[d] " Had the great body of your nation, and efpe- cially the rulers of it in the time of Chrift, em- braced Chriftianity; as it was a religion which fprung up among yourfelves, it would have been faid at this day, that it was a contrivance of thofe who had it in their power to impofe upon the com- mon people, and to make them believe whatever they pleafed; and that your fcriptures which bear teftimony to Chrift had been altered to favour the impofture. Whereas the violent oppofition which your nation in general, and the rulers of it, made to Chriftianity, will for ever put it out of the power of unbelievers to fay, that it was a fcheme which the founders of it carried on in concert with any human powers."—See the letters lately addreffed to the Jews by Dr. *Prieftly*, in which, with a force of perfuafion they ought to feel, he invites them to an amicable difcuffion with him of the evidences of Chriftianity. Fifth Letter, p. 45.

Let us now pause a moment; and endeavour to bring back our thoughts to the resurrection of *Lazarus*.—Never, except when Jesus himself rose from the dead, was a scene so interesting exhibited on the stage of this world. The consideration of it should engage us to exercise faith in Christ as our Saviour, and to rely on his power to deliver us from the all-devouring grave. His exhortation to his apostles just before his last sufferings was; *You believe in God. Believe also in me.*—Thus also, in his words, would I now exhort you.—" You believe in God." He is the ONE SUPREME, and the cause of all the causes of your happiness. " But believe also in Christ." He is the one Mediator, and the chosen Minister of God's goodness to you. *As in Adam all die; so in him shall all be made alive.* 1 Cor. xv. 22. Soon he will descend again from heaven, not to labour and suffer, but to gather the fruits of his labours and sufferings; not to die, but to destroy death, and to *change these our vile bodies,*

bodies, that they may be fashioned like unto his glorious body, according to that mighty power by which he is able to subdue all things to himself. Phil. iii. 21. *As the Father hath life in himself, so hath he given to the Son to have life in himself.* John. v. 26. We have been contemplating a striking proof of this. As his call brought Lazarus to life; so will it, hereafter, bring to life you and me and all mankind. At his coming *the sea shall give up the dead that are in it, and death and the invisible state shall give up the dead that are in them. He shall sit on the throne of his glory, and before him shall be gathered all nations to be judged according to their works.—He shall separate them as a shepherd divideth his sheep from the goats—The righteous he shall place on his right hand; the wicked on his left. To the former he will say; Come ye blessed of my father, inherit the kingdom prepared for you from the foundation of the world. To the latter, Go, ye cursed, into everlasting fire.—* God grant, fellow-christians, that we may be prepared for this solemn time. A
step

step more may bring us to it. Death is pressing hard towards us; and when it comes, the curtain will drop which hides from our view another world, and, these scenes will open upon us. The intervening time of lying amongst the dead our imaginations are apt greatly to misrepresent. There may be, to our perceptions, no difference whether it is four days, as in the case of Lazarus, or a thousand ages. Let us then be stedfast in every good purpose, never, while in the way of our duty, desponding under any troubles or weeping as without hope, forasmuch as we know *that our Redeemer liveth, and will stand at the latter day on the earth; and that though our bodies must putrify in the ground, and worms devour them, yet in our flesh we shall see God.* Job xix. 26.

And now, before I dismiss you, let me desire you to join with me, in taking one more view of what passed at Lazarus's grave. It is pleasing in the highest degree to set before our imaginations that scene.

scene.—Christ declares himself the resurrection and the life; and then walks to the grave. In his way to it (observing the sorrow of Lazarus's friends, and reflecting on the calamities of human nature) he falls into tears. When arrived at it, he orders the stone at the mouth of it to be taken away; and (in answer to Martha, who objected that the smell would be offensive) he says, that if she believed, she should see the glory of God—He solemnly addresses the Deity, and thanks him for hearing him—The spectators stand around big with expectation—He cries with a loud voice, *Lazarus come forth*—Immediately he came forth, and shewed himself alive—Conceive, if you can, the astonishment this produced. Think, particularly, of the emotions of Lazarus's friends. What delight must they have felt? How joyful must it have been to Martha and Mary to receive their beloved brother from the dead? With what ecstacies must they have embraced him, and welcomed him to to the light of life? How, probably, did they fall down before Jefus in gratitude and wonder?

But let not our thoughts ſtop here. Let us carry them on to the morning of the univerſal reſurrection. What happened now was a faint reſemblance of what will happen then.—How gladly will virtuous men open their eyes on that morning, and hail the dawning of an endleſs day? With what rapture will they then meet, congratulate one another on their eſcape from danger and trouble and unite their voices in praiſing their Deliver? What will be their joy to exchange corruption for incorruption, and weakneſs for power; to take leave of ſin and ſorrow, and loſe all their maladies; to throw off their fetters, recover perfect health and liberty, mount up on high to *meet the Lord in the air*, and draw immortal breath?

Oh! bleſſed period!—Come Lord Jeſus. Come quickly. And when thy voice

voice shall hereafter awake all the dead; may we find this happiness ours; and be taken, with all we have loved here, to live with thee for ever.

F I N I S.

www.ingramcontent.com/pod-product-compliance
Lightning Source LLC
Chambersburg PA
CBHW020303240426
43673CB00039B/686